M000113397

THE
RUGBY
POCKET BIBLE

THE
POCKET BIBLE
SERIES

THE
RUGBY
POCKET BIBLE

BEN COLES

ACKNOWLEDGEMENTS

To James Hutchison for the opportunity and Holly Ivins for her advice and patience. To my Mum, Dad and brother Fergus for their support and faith in me. And lastly to Humphrey, Oscar, Elissa and Kerry for bearing with me through the writing process.

This edition first published in Great Britain 2012 by
Crimson Publishing, a division of Crimson Business Ltd
Westminster House
Kew Road
Richmond
Surrey
TW9 2ND

A catalogue record for this book is available from the British Library.

ISBN 978 1 907087 301

Illustrations by Fergus Coles

Typeset by IDSUK (DataConnection) Ltd
Printed and bound by Lego Print SpA, Trento

CONTENTS

INTRODUCTION

To someone unfamiliar with the game, at first glance rugby can appear to be a form of organised chaos. The physicality and speed of the game are instantly appreciable, but just what is going on when all those players huddle together in two packs and drive into each other? And why are all those players on the ground falling on top of each other? And what on earth is a 'maul'? Answers to all of these questions, and many more, can be found here in *The Rugby Pocket Bible*.

Arguably, no sport shares as strong a bond between players as rugby. Players need to be aggressive but not without being smart; physical but within the code of the game; shine individually but for the gain of the team not personal glory. It is this camaraderie that has seen the game spread around the world.

Rugby tests an individual's physical capabilities to the limit, as well as their skill levels under extreme pressure from opponents. A degree of courage is required for every tackle, as is composure for every kick. Add to this the high levels of fitness required to last the 80 minutes, and you have a sport unlike any other.

The Rugby Pocket Bible examines all facets of the game, from the legends of the past who inspire today's young aspiring players, to the world's best teams, to advising you on what position would be best suited for you. There is advice on what to take on a rugby tour, where to find a club, as well as detailed examinations of the key moments in the sport's history. In short, *The Rugby Pocket Bible* has everything you want and need to know about the game.

HISTORY OF THE GAME

The history of rugby can appear to be like one great maul; from the numerous sets of rules used by different schools, clubs and countries during the early years, to the split from rugby league and Association Football, and the modern expansion of the sport. Rules, governing bodies and organisations have merged and split up, there have been heroes and scandals, glory and heartbreak, and the game is still getting bigger and better.

☺ THE INVENTOR OF THE GAME ☺

The man credited with the invention of the game is William Webb Ellis. Legend has it that during a game of football in 1823, Webb Ellis, a student at Rugby School in Warwickshire, picked up the ball and simply ran with it in his hands. Unbelievably, this simple act led to the creation of one of the biggest team sports in the world.

Although Webb Ellis never played the game as we know it today, he will always be revered as the father of the sport as the best sides in the world continue to compete for the biggest prize in the game, the World Cup trophy which bears his name.

The legend of Webb Ellis

The account of William Webb Ellis's moment of inspiration comes solely from the testimony of Matthew Holbeche Bloxam, a former Rugby School pupil, meaning that evidence for the story is far from concrete. Others have laid claim to being the

---

first person to run with the ball including Jem Mackie in 1838, a renowned physical runner. Despite the competing claims and lack of evidence, though, the story of Webb Ellis's actions, perhaps due to its romantic nature of a sudden moment of inspiration, is the one that has stuck.

DISORGANISATION OF THE RULES

The search for an alternative to the ground-based game of football begun by Webb Ellis's carrying of the ball soon saw various other leading schools in the country such as Eton, Harrow, Marlborough and Winchester all competing with their own sets of rugby rules for football. These early incarnations of rugby were remarkably different from the game we know today though; teams didn't consist of 15 players, but were instead made up of an unlimited number of bodies sometimes taking part in gigantic rucks and mauls.

This lack of regulation made it impossible for the rugby-playing schools to compete against each other, not only for those still at school but also for the former students who had enjoyed the game whilst at school and wanted to continue playing. This clashing of rules peaked during a game between Old Rugbeians and Old Etonians, spurring the Cambridge and former Rugby School student Arthur Pell to draw up a set of universal regulations called 'The Cambridge Rules' in 1848. With this set of established rules, the game flourished across the British Isles.

Over the next 20 to 30 years requests for amendments to Pell's constitution led to the need for a governing body that could maintain and enforce an agreed set of rules for clubs around the country. This led to the formation of the Rugby Football Union (see p.3).

BREAKING WITH THE FOOTBALL ASSOCIATION

It is important to remember that during its early development, rugby was very much a variation of the game of football and not an individual sport in its own right. With the growing use of running with the ball in hand rather than playing with the feet, there were glaring differences between the two sports, though, and these soon came to a head.

On 26 October 1863 a meeting, organised by Barnes FC and involving 11 clubs, took place on Great Queen Street in London. This became known as the first meeting of the Football Association.

The original plan had been to merge football rules and Rugby School rules together, but after the introduction of new rules which forbade running with the ball, it became clear that this merging of football and rugby would not happen. Blackheath, one of the teams keen to ensure there was a merger, withdrew when it became clear that this was not going to be the case, with many others following suit, leading to the development of rugby as a separate game.

⊖ FORMATION OF THE RFU ⊖

Following the break from the Football Association the need for a governing body for the game of rugby became even more pressing, and in 1871 in the Pall Mall Restaurant on Regent Street the Rugby Football Union (RFU) was born. Representatives were present from 21 clubs, many of which still exist today, including Richmond, Harlequins and Blackheath, as well as school sides such as Wellington College and St Paul's School, together with King's College, Guy's Hospital and the Civil Service.

The meeting, chaired by EC Holmes, club captain of Richmond, ruled out controversial parts of the game such as 'hacking' and 'tripping', further distinguishing the game from its football origins. The founding clubs, which were later dissolved, included some exotic names such as Mohicans, Wimbledon Hornets, Flamingoes and Gipsies.

Pocket fact H

A representative from London club Wasps was due to attend the meeting, but according to various accounts was sent to the wrong venue for the event, where he got so drunk that once he realised he was in the wrong pub, he was physically unable to direct himself to the correct venue, missing the meeting altogether.

The laws of the game that were established at the Pall Mall meeting were also taken up by various clubs north of the border in Scotland, including Glasgow Academicals, Edinburgh University, Edinburgh Academicals, Royal High School and Edinburgh Wanderers. This acceptance of the laws paved the way for the first rugby international match which was played later that same year.

⊚ FIRST INTERNATIONAL MATCH ⊚

The first ever international match was staged between the two old enemies, England and Scotland, at Raeburn Place in Edinburgh on 27 March 1871, with an attendance estimated at around 4,000. Scotland were the victors, scoring one goal and one try to England's one goal (see p.25 for an explanation of the scoring system).

According to the notes of AG Guillemard, a stalwart of the RFU who made records of matches, Scotland were the fitter and more organised side and so it proved in the second half when they began to the leave their visiting opposition behind, scoring a controversial try where the ball was held up over the ground as opposed to being touched down over the try line. Due to the confusion, the try stood, but it was the resulting fall-out over the 'try' that led to the creation of the International Rugby Board.

Pocket fact H

In 1877 the decision was made to reduce the number of players on each team from 20 to 15 in order to create less confusion on the field.

☙ FORMATION OF THE IRB ☙

Born out of a disagreement between the Scottish Rugby Union and the RFU over a controversial try in the match between England and Scotland in 1871, the International Rugby Board (IRB) has served the governing body of the sport for over 125 years.

The IRB was established in 1884 at a meeting between the four British unions in Dublin in 1886. Scotland agreed to accept that the disputed try from the first international match against England was wrong if an international body was created to govern the game with equal representation from the unions of England, Scotland, Ireland and Wales.

The official inauguration took place in Manchester that same year, but the RFU refused to comply with the rules proposed by the new organisation and as a result were exiled from international fixtures during 1888 and 1889. The matter went to court, where Lord Kingsburgh, the Lord Justice Clerk, and Major Marindin, the head of the Football Association, fully established the IRB and ensured that all international matches should be played under IRB rules and regulations.

In 1930 a full set of rules was finally fully agreed between the unions, replacing the respective home nations' rules previously used for home matches.

In 1947 New Zealand, Australia and South Africa were accepted onto the board, with France joining in 1978 and Argentina, Canada, Italy and Japan joining in 1991, finally making the board truly international.

At present, there are 118 member unions of the IRB, classified into three tiers.

- **Tier one nations:** England, Scotland, Ireland, Wales, France, Italy, Australia, New Zealand, South Africa, and Argentina.

- **Tier two nations:** Canada, Georgia, Fiji, Japan, Romania, Samoa, Tonga and the United States.

- **Tier three nations:** The remaining union members, including Russia and Portugal.

⬭ GROWING APART: THE ⬭ SEPARATION OF LEAGUE AND UNION

Despite the founding of governing bodies like the RFU and the IRB, the game endured further changes when disagreements over class and professionalism in the game divided the north and south of England.

The split came about when rugby clubs in the north which were founded by local businesses didn't deduct any pay from those workers who spent an afternoon on the pitch as opposed to at work. In essence, the businesses were paying them to play. This encouraged other players from around the region to join the sides that offered financial reward.

Following this, any payment to players was forbidden by the RFU to avoid professionalism creeping into the game. The ban was intended to ensure that no team would have an advantage over another, making the game open to any team and keeping every-one on a level playing field.

Along with payments to players, though, the clubs in the north, which received exceptional support from the public and attracted huge crowds, also began to use professional trainers. These national differences came to a head in 1893 when a meeting of the RFU was called in order to clarify the union's stance against professionalism.

Two northern representatives of the RFU, J A Miller and M Newsome of Yorkshire, both appealed for a change in the laws so that their working players would not lose any pay when playing the game, but their proposition was turned down by the panel. Representation in terms of the numbers of men playing the game was considerably higher in the north, but this could not sway the vote as more southerners dominated the RFU Committee. This disagreement and the result of the vote then led to the departure of the 22 leading Lancashire and Yorkshire clubs to form the Northern Union.

THE NORTHERN UNION

The end result was the formation of the Northern Union in August 1895. Huddersfield, Batley, Dewsbury, Bradford, Manningham, Leeds, Halifax, Brighouse Rangers, Hull, Liversedge, Hunslet and Wakefield broke away from the RFU to create the new organisation, with 10 more joining before the first round of matches on 7 September 1895.

By the start of the next season nearly 60 sides were participating when the Challenge Cup was introduced, with the first title being won by Batley against St Helens on 1 May 1897. The Northern Union blossomed at an impressive rate, with nearly 14,000 people attending the Cup game, and ticket sales totalling £620, indicating that the game could be run successfully without the aid of the RFU and making the move for independence appear increasingly more credible.

This early success would ultimately provide the foundations of the game of rugby league, while the remaining clubs continued to play for free in what became known as rugby union.

Pocket fact H

According to the RFU and the Guinness Book of Records *the oldest rugby club in the world is Guy's Hospital RFC which was founded in 1843. The club produced 34 internationals between 1872 and 1970, and its first match was played on Blackheath Common in the 1850s. In the 1980s, Guy's Hospital merged with St Thomas's Hospital and as a consequence so did the two rugby clubs. Now the club puts out sides in the British Universities and Colleges Sport (BUCS) leagues and in the Kent Metropolitan League.*

☉ THE AGE OF PROFESSIONALISM ☉

It wasn't until 100 years after the split from the northern teams that rugby union finally turned professional. There had been an obvious divide between the two games as an increasing number of rugby union players switched over to rugby league for substantial salaries. As a result, rugby union failed to keep up and underwent several accusations of 'shamateurism' when top players were made payments in the form of trust funds and other such means. The IRB were left with no choice but to make the game professional in order to prevent any further scandal and they declared the game 'open' on 26 August 1995.

Deciding whether professionalism has been a success remains a debatable topic. Whilst tournaments like the Heineken Cup and Super Rugby have flourished during the professional era, there have been plenty of casualties along the way. Many of the most famous and oldest English clubs have crumbled under the financial pressures of the professional age, including Richmond, Orrell, Wakefield and London Scottish, forcing them to disband and start from scratch.

That being said, without professionalism, rugby union would have fallen well behind not only its closest competitor rugby league, but also cricket and football. The change may not have been universally desired, but it was absolutely necessary.

Pocket fact H

Just after rugby union went professional in 1995, it was thought that the two codes should be more harmonious and so Bath and Wigan played a two-match series against each other, with one game in each code.

⊖ IMPORTANT FIRSTS ⊖

First Welsh club

Rugby was first set up in Wales at Lampeter College in 1850.

First Irish club

The first club to be formed in Ireland was at Trinity College Dublin in 1854 by English students who had played the game at school.

First Scottish club

Edinburgh Academy (Edinburgh Academical Football Club) was the first club to be formed in Scotland in 1857.

Pocket fact H

The first team founded outside the UK was at Neuenheim College in Heidelberg, Germany, in 1850.

First rugby club in New Zealand

The first rugby club in New Zealand was the Nelson Football Club, founded in 1868 by Robert Collings Tennent. Tennent moved from England to New Zealand with his mother in 1865 and took the game that he had played as a schoolboy with him. However, it was Charles Monro, who had been educated at Christ College, Finchley, in England who introduced the rugby rules to Nelson Football Club when he returned to New Zealand at the age of 19 in 1870. The first competitive game of rugby was played two years after the club's foundation on 14 May 1870.

First rugby cup

Contested between the six medical schools in London, the United Hospitals Cup has been in existence since 1874. The first final was held in March 1875 at the Oval. It was won by Guy's Hospital, who defeated St George's Hospital in front of 400 spectators by a converted try and one try, to two tries. The tournament has been played annually with no interruption except during the war years in the last century.

First international trophy

The oldest trophy in the game, the Calcutta Cup, is named after a match played in Calcutta, India, on Christmas Day in 1872 between 20 players representing England and 20 players representing Scotland, Wales and Ireland. The first match for the cup was played between Scotland and England at Raeburn Place in Edinburgh in 1879 and ended in a draw. The first winners were

England who won in Manchester the following year by two tries and three goals to one goal. England have won the trophy 64 times, Scotland 39 times, and 15 of their encounters have ended in a draw.

Pocket fact H

During the original All Blacks tour to the British Isles, France and the United States of America in 1905, the touring side performed the haka (a traditional war dance) before their matches, a tradition that continues today. On the advice of Welsh Rugby Union administrator Tom Williams, when Wales faced the All Blacks at Cardiff Arms Park in front of 47,000 supporters, Wales' Teddy Morgan responded to the haka by singing Hen Wlad Fy Nhadau (Land of my Fathers), *the Welsh national anthem. The crowd soon joined in, in effect creating the first national anthem at a sporting event.*

First Home Nations Championship

More than a decade after the first international match between England and Scotland, the first Home Nations Championship took place in 1883 between England, Scotland, Ireland and Wales. Held from December through to March, matches took place at Whalley Range in Manchester, Raeburn Place in Edinburgh, Ormeau Road in Belfast and at St Helen's rugby ground in Swansea. Matches were decided by whichever side had the highest number of goals (a successful conversion, or a dropped goal, or a penalty goal), with tries only being tallied if no goals were scored. The winners were England who also won the Triple Crown by beating all three of the other nations involved.

First rugby sevens tournament

The first ever rugby sevens tournament took place in Melrose, Scotland, in 1883. The idea came from two local butchers, Ned Haig and David Sanderson, who devised the format for a fund-raising event at Melrose Rugby Club. Reducing the team from

15 players to seven was principally done for entertainment purposes and the event featured seven local sides, Melrose, Gala, Selkirk, St Cuthbert's, Earlston, St Ronan's and Gala Forest.

Melrose won the final against Gala but under controversial circumstances, leaving the field after scoring a try but allegedly before the allocated time had been used up. The competition has now been running for 128 years and Hawick Rugby Club is the most successful in the competition's history with 28 wins.

First overseas tour

The first tour away from the British Isles took place in 1888, when an unofficial party of players from England, Ireland, Scotland and Wales travelled to New Zealand and Australia.

The tour was not backed by the RFU but was allowed to go ahead providing that it didn't conflict with the rules of amateurism imposed by the Union. The side played in red, white and blue-hooped jerseys with white shorts. Led by England's Robert Seddon from Swinton, the touring party played a total of 35 matches, winning 27, drawing six and losing just two.

Pocket fact H

In the same year that the first British side toured New Zealand and Australia, a New Zealand side consisting of players of Maori and Pakeha origin toured Britain, New Zealand and Australia. This tour also proved to be the longest ever as the New Zealand Natives played 107 matches, winning 78, drawing six, and losing 23.

First domestic league

While many countries operated unofficial championships until the 1970s, the French National Rugby Championship has existed since 1892. Now known as the Top 14, the first final was contested between Stade Français and Racing Club in 1892. Won 4–3 by Racing, the match was played at Bagatelle in Paris in front of 2,000 spectators. The most successful side in the competition are Stade Toulousain, with a record 18 titles.

First World Cup in 1987

Held in New Zealand and Australia, the first ever Rugby World Cup featured a total of 16 nations, from established teams such as the Home Nations to relative minnows like Japan, Zimbabwe and the United States. South Africa were excluded from the tournament due to the ongoing state of apartheid in the country.

The majority of matches were played at nine venues in New Zealand, while stadiums in Brisbane and Sydney in Australia hosted group stage matches, as well as quarter and semi-final games in Brisbane. The estimated overall attendance was over 600,000 and matches were played between 22 May and 20 June. The winners were New Zealand who won the final against France at Eden Park in Auckland by an emphatic 29–9.

Pocket fact H

Western Samoa, who had been in impressive form leading up to the tournament, were bizarrely excluded from the first World Cup. This was arguably due to their lack of international matches away from Samoa, but no official reason was given by the IRB.

◉ STATE OF THE MODERN GAME ◉

Today, rugby union sees 94 nations appearing on the IRB World Rankings, from traditional powerhouses such as England, South Africa and France to up and coming sides like Tahiti, Guam and Vanuatu. And the sport continues to grow.

VITAL STATISTICS OF RUGBY UNION

- **19%:** according to research by Mastercard Worldwide carried out in April 2011, overall global participation has risen by 19% since the 2007 Rugby World Cup.

- **5,000,000:** rugby is now the first-choice sport for five million men, women and children in over 117 countries. The key to this increase comes from the growth in participation amongst the emerging nations, up 18% in Asia, 33% in Africa and 22% in South America.

- **800,000,000 and 500,000:** the growth in figures between the 2003 and 2007 World Cups, which saw an increase of 800 million in TV viewing figures and 500,000 for the total attendance.

VITAL STATISTICS OF RUGBY LEAGUE

- **19,200,000:** the 2008 Rugby League World Cup was the biggest event in the sport's history, attracting a global television audience of 19.2 million.

- **40:** rugby league is played today in over 40 countries around the world, both professionally and semi-professionally.

- **285,000:** the number of players registered across the UK currently sits at nearly 300,000.

See p.55 for more on rugby league.

Pocket fact H

The first known streaker at a sporting event was Australian Michael O'Brien, who ran out onto the pitch naked during a Test match between England and France at Twickenham in 1974. PC Bruce Perry used his helmet to spare O'Brien's modesty, and the helmet is now preserved in the rugby museum at Twickenham.

2

RULES OF THE GAME

Understanding all of the rules in rugby union can be a bit of a challenge, but the basic concept of the game is quite simple. The aim is to touch the ball down over your opponent's try line. Getting there, however, is not easy. This chapter outlines the rules you have to obey to get to that try line.

⊖ THE BASICS ⊖

A game of rugby lasts 80 minutes, split into two 40-minute halves. The team with the highest number of points at the end of the match wins, and these points are scored through tries, penalties, drop goals and conversions (see p.25 for more).

A rugby team is made up of 15 players in two groups: eight forwards and seven backs. Within these two sets of players there are different groups based on the formation of the scrum (see p.17). In the forwards are the front row – made up of two props and one hooker; two second rows, and three back row forwards – made up of two flankers and one number 8. In the backs there are also three groups of players: the half-backs (a scrum-half and a fly-half); the centres (an inside and outside centre); and lastly the back three (two wingers and a full back). (See p.42 for an explanation of positions.)

⊖ PASSING ⊖

Rugby's key difference from Association Football (aside from handling the ball) is that it is against the rules to pass in a forward motion. A forward pass results in a scrum being awarded to the opposition team. By passing backwards, teams look to move up the pitch either through breaking tackles or by managing to run through any gaps available.

Passes are regularly dispatched in a spiral motion, so that the ball travels more directly and is easier to catch. Players use their strong hand, normally their writing hand, to provide the power behind the ball whilst using their weaker hand to guide the direction of the pass. However, given that it is not always possible to produce a spiral pass under extreme pressure, there are other variations.

- **A pop pass** is carried out using a flicking motion of the hands either into space in front of another player running on to the ball or from one man to the other when there is little space on offer.

- **A dive pass** is normally used by scrum-halves at the bases of rucks and scrums in order to speed up possession, or when they are under extreme pressure. This pass is sometimes attempted by other less nimble members of the team such as props, to varying levels of effect.

⬤ TACKLING ⬤

One of rugby's more famous aspects, tackling is not only a crowd pleaser but also sets the game apart from other sports. Rugby is well-known for its big hits, and as the players have become bigger in recent years, so have the tackles.

There are several regulations dictating when and how a tackle can be made. For safety reasons, players are not permitted to tackle the opposition if they do not have the ball, or if they are in the air. Tackles must also be made below the neck, so as to avoid any serious injury.

Once tackled, the player must release the ball when he hits the ground. This is done by placing the ball back in the direction of his team, where a ruck (see p.20) is then formed in order to protect the ball from the opposition. The scrum-half or forwards then begin the next phase of play by picking up the ball and either passing or running with it.

However, the tackler does have the opportunity to try and rip the ball away from the tackled player before the ball is played, but only until the ruck is formed. Other more cynical forms of stopping the opposition, such as pushing, tripping with the legs, or charging with the shoulder, are also against the rules, and can result in yellow or red cards.

Pocket fact H

There are forms of rugby which are played without tackling, namely touch rugby and tag rugby (see p. 59 for more).

⊜ ELEMENTS OF THE GAME ⊜

THE SCRUM

One of the sport's most iconic passages of play, the scrum is world-famous. The sight and sound of rugby's biggest eight players grunting their way into position before trying to out-muscle their similarly stocky opponents is one of the most enduring images of the game.

History

- The scrum evolved from the ruck, as referees needed a way to restart the game when the ball became unplayable.

- The 1888–89 New Zealand Native Team and 1905 All Blacks were two of the pioneering sides when it came to the first scrum positions, operating a seven-man 2-3-2 formation. Other nations experimented with their scrum formations, with South Africa using a 3-4-1 formation in the 1920s.

- England pack leader Wavell Wakefield in 1923 set a precedent by assigning positions to the players in the pack that are still used today, creating props and second rows. Wakefield's positions led to a Grand Slam.

- A law passed in 1931 by the IRB stipulated that all scrums must have three men in the front row.

- In the 1960s, laws were passed stating that flankers had to stay bound until the ball left the back of the scrum. In addition to this number 8s were allowed to detach with the ball.

- After years of serious and occasionally fatal incidents, in 2007 the IRB implemented laws which require props to 'crouch, touch, pause and engage' when forming a scrum. The laws also reduced the distance between the two sets of forwards upon engagement.

- In 2009, in a bid to reduce uncontested scrums, match-day squads were expanded from 22 to 23, allowing for an extra prop on the bench.

Formation

The modern-day scrum is made up of three sections.

- **The front row:** two props (loosehead and tighthead) and one hooker.

- **The second row:** two lock forwards.

- **The back row:** two flankers (blindside and openside) and a number 8.

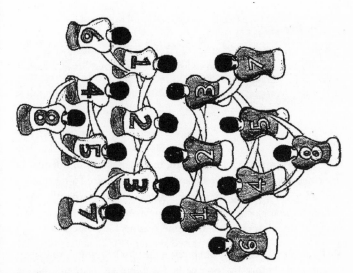

Formation of the scrum

The front and second rows link arms, with the front row standing and the second row kneeling behind them. The two flankers join onto the sides of the second rows when the front row prepares to engage, with the number 8 doing the same from the back. Both packs of forwards then follow the referee's instructions.

- The players are bound together standing up. Next, the front row follows the direction of the referee by first following the call to 'crouch'.

- Then the props and hookers 'touch' their opposite man, grabbing on to the shirt around the outside shoulder area.

- With the second rows now locked in between the props and hookers, the flankers bound on to the sides and the number 8 braced at the back, the referee will call 'pause' to check that the scrum is ready.

- When he is happy with the positioning of both packs, the referee will say 'engage', and the two packs will move forward and make contact.

Pocket fact H

Before the modern directives of 'crouch, touch, pause, engage' were introduced, players would simply throw themselves into each other on the blow of the referee's whistle, leading to many serious neck injuries.

Offences

Given the complexity of the scrum, there are plenty of offences in the rulebook. Scrums in recent times have acquired a reputation for being a burden to the game when they are constantly reset, although the majority of resets are primarily for the wellbeing and safety of the players. Here are some reasons for a reset.

- **Early engagement:** when one side's pack attempts to engage too early before the referee has said 'engage'. A combination of adrenaline and excitement for the hit means some players just cannot wait to get stuck in.

- **Boring in:** when the front rows engage at an angle. Both sets of forwards must engage in a straight line, as engaging at a different angle can sometimes give them an advantage such as restricting the hooker's movement or wheeling the scrum (turning the scrum).

- **Dropping the bind:** both sets of props must keep their bind on the shoulder of the opposite man's shirt throughout the scrum until the ball has gone. Dropping the bind can cause the scrum to collapse, which is very dangerous, resulting in a penalty to the opposition.

- **Early detachment:** flankers and number 8s must stay bound until the scrum has ended. Disengaging early results in a penalty.

- **Collapsing the scrum:** as with a maul, any attempt to try and pull the scrum down under pressure results in a penalty.

'Cauliflower ears'

The principal victims of cauliflower ears are the players in the scrum who, through constantly bashing and rubbing their ears against other players, gradually tear and bruise the ear, resulting in a blood clot and an excess of fluid. As the clot slowly wears away the cartilage in the ear starts to shrivel up, meaning it begins to resemble a cauliflower.

When are scrums awarded?

A scrum is awarded to a team after the following incidents.

- **A knock-on:** when the ball goes forward off the hands of the player in possession.

- **A forward pass:** as players are only permitted to pass backwards, a forward pass also results in a scrum to the opposition, where the other team is awarded the put-in of the ball.

- **Accidental offside:** if the ball accidentally strikes a player who is found in an offside position (ie in front of the ball), then the opposition wins a scrum.

Teams are also given the option of a scrum when a penalty is awarded to them by the referee. In areas such as the opposition's 22 or near the try line, a scrum can prove to be a very effective weapon.

Pocket fact H

For the first two years of their existence New Zealand played in navy-blue jerseys but they decided on an all-black strip for their 1905 tour to the UK as Scotland also played in navy and the tourists could only afford one set of kit.

THE RUCK

Arguably the source of more penalty infringements than any other area of the game, the ruck is also key to both retaining and turning over opposition balls. Rucks can sometimes look like chaos, but there is a method to the madness.

- A ruck forms when two players from each side bind together over the ball and attempt to force each other backwards.

- The players bind in a position that is similar to that of the scrum, crouching and leaning over the ball in order to drive up with the legs.

- After the ruck has formed, other players must join from behind the primary players, ie from 'the back foot'. Players who join the ruck from the side are penalised with a straight penalty.

- In order not to 'kill' the ball (by lying on it), players have to stay on their feet. If they become unbalanced and are knocked down, then they must attempt to roll away.

- Use of the hands in the ruck is illegal. Players must use their feet to move the ball back towards their team.

- With 'quick' ball potentially being so dangerous for a defence, defending players will often try to slow down the ball by lying over it or covering it with their hands but without being detected by the referee. Some will pretend that they simply cannot move in an attempt to trick the referee.

- Occasionally, the ball may be impossible to retrieve, resulting in the awarding of a scrum to whichever side the referee deems to have the forward momentum at the ruck.

Pocket fact H

Richmond became the first club to sign a player for £1 million when they captured Ben Clarke from Bath in 1996. The fee was financed by their millionaire backer Ashley Levett, but this proved to be an unsustainable precedent as Levett placed Richmond into administration in March 1999.

THE MAUL

A maul is one of the most powerful moves found in rugby. Mauls either occur in open play or after a lineout, when one man is tackled and remains standing on his feet. When done correctly, mauls can be incredibly effective, especially when attacking in the opposition's 22 (see diagram p.40), given that defences are either rumbled back out of the way or concede penalties in attempting to stop the maul.

- For the maul to be formed, another teammate binds onto the man in possession, after which others also bind on. As in a ruck, this has to happen from the back foot of the last player to bind on, not from the side.

- As many players as possible can join the maul as long as it carries on moving.

- If a maul comes to a halt and the ball is not played either by the man with possession running off the back or passing the ball, then a scrum is awarded to the opposing side.

- It is illegal for the opposition to pull down the maul at any stage. Doing so will result in a penalty to the side in possession.

- Mauls can be very effective if carried out successfully, because the man at the back is protected with the ball whilst the players in front drive forward. Mauls can technically go on until the try line if the opposition is not strong enough to stop them.

- The attacking side must also ensure that the ball carrier is positioned at the back of the maul and does not detach from the bound players in front of him. Doing so results in an offence often referred to as 'truck-and-trailer' (see Glossary, p.180), and either a scrum or a penalty is awarded to the opposition, depending on whether the break was accidental or not.

THE MARK

An aspect of the game that is similar to Australian Rules Football, rugby players can call the mark when they catch the ball from a kick within their own 22 area. In the past players could call for a mark anywhere across the field, but from the 1970s the rules have changed meaning that a mark can only be called within the defending side's 22.

Once the mark has been called by shouting the word 'mark', the opposition are not allowed to tackle the player who has made the call. The catcher then has three options: to take a kick, tap the ball and run, or have a scrum. Marks cannot be called from a kick-off as they would damage the free-flowing nature of the game.

THE LINEOUT

A facet of the game that has developed rapidly over the years, the lineout in the modern game requires great athleticism and bravery. Whereas decades ago height played a crucial factor in winning lineouts as there was no lifting, in the modern game it requires athletic jumpers and lifters, as well as tactical calls, in order to create a consistently effective lineout.

Teams traditionally use up to three jumpers, at the front, middle and back of the lineout, working in pods of two lifters and one jumper. In order to confuse the opposition so that they cannot compete for the ball, jumpers and lifters may move up and down the line before the ball is thrown in. Once the ball is thrown in the lifters will lift the designated jumper who will attempt to take the ball cleanly.

History

Whilst rugby league abolished the lineout in 1897, it has remained part of the game in rugby union. Traditionally, both sets of forwards would simply stand in two lines and jump for the ball, without any lifting of players. This continued until the 1980s, when lifting was allegedly first trialled by Bernard Millington, a Trafford MV RFCC player.

The call

In recent times, following the introduction of lifters in the lineout, this area of the game has become as much a mental battle as a physical one. Teams will now have a lineout leader who will make the calls on each attacking lineout to signal which 'play' his team should carry out.

Teams can have as many types of lineout calls as they please, normally working on the basis of a set code, such as the names of animals. Teams strive to make the calls as complex as possible, so that the opposition cannot crack the code and work out where the ball is going to be thrown in, which would give them a better chance of stealing possession.

Formation

A lineout happens when the ball goes into touch on either the left-hand or right-hand side of the field. From this point, the hooker for the side which will take the lineout will retrieve the ball from off the field and position himself on the mark from where the ball went out.

- The two sides will walk over to the lineout, lining up on whichever half of the pitch they are playing, with the attacking side making a decision on which lineout play they plan to carry out.

- The attacking side decides the numbers of players in the lineout, with the opposition having to match the numbers themselves. Failing to do so results in a free kick to the other side.

- The two teams must stand in two straight lines, 5 metres in from where the hooker throws the ball and with a 1-metre gap between the two lines.

- As the hooker motions to throw the ball in, the two sides lift the jumpers into the air to contest the ball. Lifting is traditionally done by two players, but sometimes only one lifter is used to free up more forwards in the lineout either to create additional pods or to break from the lineout more quickly.

- When a player catches the ball, they will either pass the ball down to the scrum-half or keep it in their hands and bring it down in order to set up a maul. Once the player touches the ground, the opposition may compete for the ball by tackling the man.

Pocket fact H

Introduced in 2009 with the ELVs (Experimental Law Variations, see p.35 for more on this), a quick lineout is when any player passes the ball from off the pitch infield over 5 metres to another man, throwing the ball either flat or backwards, before the lineout has been formed. It was introduced to speed up the flow of the game and has proved a great success.

Formation of a lineout

Offences

- Players are not permitted to be lifted into the air before the hooker begins to throw the ball in. An early lift results in a free kick to the opposition.

- The hooker must make sure that the ball is thrown in straight down the channel between the two lines of forwards. Hookers will of course try to edge the ball towards their teammates in order to help them retain possession, but the trick is to do so without drawing the attention of the referee.

- Players are not allowed to interfere with the other jumpers when they are in the air, for safety reasons. Any attempt to knock or pull the other man out of the air will result in a penalty.

- Any players who are not part of the lineout when it is formed must wait 10 metres behind the lineout, apart from the scrum-half. They must wait until the ball has passed the 15-metre line. Advancing too early results in a penalty to the opposition.

⊖ SCORING ⊖

Throughout rugby's history, the complicated scoring system has continued to change. With no universal code for rugby until the late 19th and early 20th centuries, certain club sides, regions and national teams operated using very different methods for calculating who the winner of each match was. However, since 1992, matches have been decided by the following universal scoring system.

TRY

Today the most profitable way of earning points in a rugby match, tries are now worth five points.

Tries are scored by grounding the ball within the opposition's try area. Downward pressure is necessary for a try to be given by the referee. Players can score tries by either placing the ball down themselves with their hands and arms, or, if the ball is loose on the ground, by diving on top of it and applying downward pressure with the hands or arms. Placing the ball against the base of the post also counts as a try to the attacking side.

Pocket fact H

A try derives its name from the game's past, when a kick for the posts was worth more than scoring a try, so players would 'try' to place the ball over the line in order to get a shot at goal.

PENALTY TRY

In the event that the defensive team continually infringes near to their own try line, such as being offside, taking out the man without the ball, or persistent offences at the scrum, then the referee will award a penalty try to the attacking side, worth the same number of points as a normal try. The conversion is taken from in front of the posts.

Pocket fact H

Back in 1891, tries were only worth one point, meaning they were the least valuable means of scoring. Conversions, penalties and drop goals were all worth more.

CONVERSION

Following the scoring of a try, the team's kicker takes a conversion to add a further two points to his team's tally. This is achieved by kicking the ball through the posts. The conversion is taken horizontally in line with where the try was scored, and can be taken from as far forward or as far back in a vertical line from where the try was scored as the kicker wants in order to increase or decrease the angle towards the posts.

Pocket fact H

The highest conversion points scorer is fly-half Dan Carter of New Zealand, with more than 220 conversions, making 440 points.

PENALTY KICK

After the referee has awarded a penalty to a team, they have the option of kicking at goal. The player must kick the ball off the ground, balancing it on either a tee or sand, and must kick at goal from the mark where the penalty is awarded. Three points are awarded if the ball is kicked through the posts.

Pocket fact H

The record for the longest ever penalty kick in rugby is held by Paul Thorburn, with a 64.2-metre kick when playing for Wales against Scotland in the 1986 Home Nations Championship.

DROP GOALS

Also worth three points, drop goals are scored when a player drops the ball on the ground and kicks it through the posts during the normal run of play. Drop goals can be taken from anywhere on the pitch. Sometimes used as a last resort in order to snatch points with little time left on the clock, drop goals have led to many famous victories.

Pocket fact H

England fly-half Jonny Wilkinson holds the record for the most drop goals at international level, with 36.

⊖ SUBSTITUTIONS ⊖

Since the introduction of a rule on substitutions was passed in 1968, the number allowed has gradually increased from the original three to the seven or eight that are now permitted. The IRB ruled that each side must have two substitutes per match.

The number of substitutes available to each side currently varies around the world. The domestic leagues in the northern hemisphere, such as the Aviva Premiership in England, the Celtic League and Top 14 League in France, all have match-day squads of 23, including eight substitutes. However, in international matches, and in Super Rugby and European competitions such as the Heineken Cup and Amlin Challenge Cup, only seven substitutes are permitted.

Substitutions are made once the fourth official on the touchline has communicated with the referee that a team wants to bring on a substitute. There is no limit on how many substitutes can be used in a match, and teams are able to bring on their entire bench if necessary.

BLOOD SUBSTITUTIONS

If a player is bleeding, then teams must make what is called a blood substitution, where the wounded player is made to leave the field to receive treatment. Teams can send on a replacement while the wounded player is off the pitch.

Bloodgate scandal

During the 2009 Heineken Cup quarter-final between Harlequins and Leinster at The Stoop in Twickenham, Harlequins winger Tom Williams left the field with an alleged cut lip. He was replaced by specialist kicker and fly-half Nick Evans, who unsuccessfully tried to win Harlequins the match with a drop goal in the dying minutes.

The cut on Williams' lip turned out to be fake, and it emerged that Harlequins physiotherapist Steph Brennan had used a fake blood capsule to feign Williams' injury. The repercussions were severe: Williams was banned from playing for four months, Harlequins director of rugby Dean Richards was banned for three years and Brennan banned for two years. Club doctor Wendy Chapman, who then tried to cover up the fake injury to Williams by cutting his lip, was suspended by the General Medical Council. The club was also fined a total of £260,000.

⬭ FOULS ⬭

Here is a list of don'ts that will make a player feel the wrath of the crowd, their teammates or the referee.

KNOCK-ON

Perhaps the most embarrassing mistake one can make on a rugby field, a knock-on is the term for when a player in possession loses the ball forward off his hands or arms. Knock-ons commonly happen when being tackled, from the force of the hit or when the opposition try to rip the ball away. A knock-on can also result from a failure to receive a pass cleanly from a teammate.

Players can be penalised with a straight penalty for a 'deliberate' knock-on, where a player purposely knocks the ball forward in order to prevent a try or to stop an attack.

FORWARD PASS

Similar to the knock-on, a scrum is awarded to the side without the ball when the team in possession commits a forward pass. The referee or the linesman calls these.

Pocket fact H

History has seen many famous forward passes go undetected with monumental results, including the 2007 World Cup quarter-final between France and New Zealand where the winning score from Yannick Jauzion resulted from a blatant, but undetected, forward pass from Damien Traille to knock favourites New Zealand out of the tournament once again.

OFFSIDE

The offside rule in rugby union is arguably far simpler than in football. Working on a similar basis as the idea of not allowing a forward pass, players are not allowed to be positioned ahead of the ball-carrier at any time.

In defence, teams are required to work behind the offside line. If a defender rushes up too quickly before the ball has been played from the ruck, then they are offside, with a penalty being given to the attacking team.

Players are also offside when the ball is kicked ahead by one player and if a team-mate gets to the ball ahead of the kicker. All the attacking players must run behind the player who kicked the ball.

HIGH AND DANGEROUS TACKLES

According to IRB laws any tackles made above the line of the shoulders are deemed dangerous. Given that rugby players are at the most risk when tackled around the neck or head, players face harsh punishments if they commit a serious tackle. Week-long bans are also a possibility if the player is cited following the match.

'Stiff-arm tackling' is not permitted. This is where the tackler fails to wrap his arms around the ball-carrier, with the force of the swinging arm acting more like a punch.

'Spear tackling' is strictly forbidden. This is when the tackler tackles the player by lifting him into the air and then dropping him on the ground upside down, so that he lands on his head or neck. Spear tackles can lead to dislocations, spinal cord damage or broken bones in the neck area.

The O'Driscoll/Umaga/Mealamu incident

In the first test of the 2005 Lions Tour, Lions captain Brian O'Driscoll was taken out off the ball at a ruck by a two-man spear tackle from All Blacks captain Tana Umaga and hooker Keven Mealamu just 90 seconds into the match. The Lions captain was forced to leave the field with a dislocated shoulder and ruled out of the rest of the tour. The incident was picked up by television cameras but not by the authorities, causing outrage around the world.

STAMPING

Rugby players walk a very fine line when it comes to use of the boot. By law, teams are allowed to 'encourage' an opposition player to move away from the ball if he is blocking their access to it. However, occasionally the use of the boot goes too far, leading to what is known as stamping.

Pocket fact H

Quillan flanker Gaston Riviere tragically died as a result of injuries from stamping during a match against Perpignan in 1927.

BITING

One of the most dangerous and despicable acts that can be committed on a rugby field, any biting will result in an immediate red card and a lengthy ban.

Pocket fact H

Johan Le Roux received an 18-month ban from the game in 1994 after biting New Zealand hooker and captain Sean Fitzpatrick's ear in the scrum. Le Roux famously commented, 'For an 18-month suspension, I feel I probably should have torn it off'.

GOUGING

The horrendous act of gouging unfortunately still exists in the game today, with severe punishments from the game's governing bodies. Gouging is when one player makes contact with an opposition's eye or the area around the eye in order to either temporarily or permanently blind them. The punishment is a red card and multi-week ban.

Pocket fact H

Stade Français prop David Attoub was banned for 70 weeks after being found guilty of gouging opponent Stephen Ferris of Ulster in 2010.

Brawling

In such a full-on contact sport, the outpouring of aggression can sometimes go a little too far. Here are the three worst incidents of fighting seen on a rugby pitch.

The '99' Call

Willie John McBride's 1974 Lions were unbeaten on their tour of South Africa for many reasons, but one of the main reasons was their sheer aggression on the field. If one player was attacked by a South African opponent, the call of '99' would ring out, and the whole Lions team would retaliate, resulting in a mass brawl. It meant the Lions sent out a message that they would not be intimidated, but also meant that no one player could be sent off as they were all involved.

McRae's Blitz

Another incident on a Lions tour, this time in Australia in 2001, was between the Lions' Ronan O'Gara and New South Wales full-back Duncan McRae. In an off-the-ball incident following a ruck, McRae unleashed a barrage of punches on O'Gara, 11 in total, to the player's face, forcing him to leave the field. McRae was sent off by the referee and given a seven-week ban.

Champ's Knockout

When his fellow French countryman Serge Blanco received plenty of rough stuff from the England team during a Rugby World Cup warm-up match in 1991, flanker Eric Champ finally decided enough was enough. After England winger Nigel Heslop made yet another late hit on Blanco, the Frenchman (described as 'old mad eyes himself'), landed a monster punch on Heslop, knocking him out.

◉ PENALTIES ◉

When a referee decides that a penalty is not enough, he can go one step further in punishing whoever has committed an indiscretion.

YELLOW CARDS

Association Football referee Ken Aston famously devised the idea of penalising players with red and yellow cards while waiting at a set of traffic lights following the 1966 World Cup quarter-final between England and Argentina. Rugby adopted the card system using the same framework as football, with two yellows resulting in a sending off.

Yellow cards are most commonly issued as a caution following repeat offences by a player or side, with the referee having previously warned the player or captain of the side. Yellow cards might be also issued when an offence is committed by a defensive side near the try line, including repeated collapsing of the scrum, 'killing the ball' in the ruck area, tackling the man early or deliberately knocking the ball on. Yellow cards are also handed out for high or dangerous tackles, depending on the severity of the incident.

RED CARDS

Either issued as a second yellow card or as a straight card, a red card means that a player is sent off and must leave the field immediately. Unlike Association Football, red cards are rare in rugby, particularly with the two yellow card rule.

Straight red cards are normally issued for serious foul play, including dangerous tackles, gouging, biting and also brawling.

Pocket fact H

Nathan Hines (Scotland) and Marco Bortolami (Italy) both hold the worst disciplinary record at international level, with five yellow cards and one red card each.

THE SIN-BIN

Rugby's very own version of the naughty step, the sin-bin was first conceived as a 'cooler' period by South African referee Bertie Strasheim in the 1960s. Yellow cards still meant just a warning up to the 1999 World Cup, when the sin-bin became law. Now, on receiving a yellow card from the referee, players are sent to the bin for 10 minutes, reducing their side to 14 men. After their time on the sidelines is up, they are allowed to return to the field.

Pocket fact H

The first ever player to be sin-binned was Argentina's Roberto Grau, during the 1999 World Cup match with Wales at the Millennium Stadium.

⊖ THE IRB AND LAW-MAKING ⊖

Since its conception in the 1880s the IRB's influence on the laws of the game has grown as more national unions have become members. Their primary purpose (until the experimental law variations, or ELVs, were introduced in 2008) was to create a universal system by which all games were played, so that there would be no debate over alleged scores or questionable refereeing decisions. The other priority was that of safety. By creating rules that prevented any risk of serious injury, the game would be made more accessible to everyone.

Any changes to the laws of the game are first discussed by the IRB's committee then proposed to the IRB Council for inclusion in the modern game. The final decisions are made by the 26 council members with the chairman and vice-chairman Bill Beaumont and Bernard Lapasset, who add the laws into the game.

☻ THE EXPERIMENTAL LAW ☻ VARIATIONS (ELVS)

As a sport continually seeking to try and attract new fans and interest from around the world, the IRB has continued to review the state of the game after big events. For example in 2004, following the undoubted success of the 2003 World Cup in Australia, the IRB sought to examine areas where the game could be improved to make it more free-flowing and entertaining for spectators.

An investigation at a conference in Auckland held after the 2003 tournament prompted the review of the game by the IRB council. The review led to the proposition of trialling some Experimental Law Variations, which began globally from August 2008. There were 13 ELVs in total.

REFEREES

● Assistant referees are able to assist the referee in any way that the referee requires.

MAUL

● Players are able to defend a maul by pulling it down.

● Players are now allowed to enter with their head and shoulders lower than their hips.

LINEOUT AND TOUCH

● If a team puts the ball back into its own 22 and the ball is subsequently kicked directly into touch, there is no gain in ground.

● A quick throw-in may be thrown in straight or towards the throwing team's own goal line.

● There is no restriction on the number of players from either team who can participate in the lineout.

● The receiver at the lineout must be 2 metres away from the lineout.

- The player who is in opposition to the player throwing in the ball must stand in the area between the 5-metre line and the touchline but must be 2 metres away from the 5-metre line.

- Lineout players may pre-grip a jumper before the ball is thrown in.

- The lifting of lineout players is permitted.

SCRUM

- Introduction of an offside line 5 metres behind the hindmost feet of the scrum.

- Identification of scrum-half offside lines.

CORNER POSTS

- The corner posts are no longer considered to be touch-in-goal except when the ball is grounded against the post.

WERE THE ELVS SUCCESSFUL?

The majority of the rule variations had little effect on the overall game. For example, players were already being lifted in the line-out, and lifters were also gripping their jumpers before the ball was thrown in anyway. Others were great ideas; for example having the assistant referees able to help the referee whenever it was needed, if they had spotted any foul play or whether a try had been scored, made perfect sense and meant that more decisions would be made correctly.

REACTION

The reaction from the leading figures in the game towards the ELVs was mixed, to say the least. Given the success of the 2007 World Cup there was some doubt about whether the game needed to be altered at all. Once the rules had been trialled globally, some past and present players and coaches, including the most capped All Black of all time, Sean Fitzpatrick, and Springbok winger Bryan Habana, said they feared the lack of breaks in play would have a detrimental effect on the game being accessible to everyone because of the high levels of fitness and athleticism required.

Despite these reservations, the majority of the revised laws were passed and are used in the game today.

Pocket fact H

In 2003, the 7th Underwater Rugby World Championship was held in Denmark, with Sweden winning the title.

3

ESSENTIALS OF THE GAME

There are certain aspects of the game of rugby that are essential for a match to take place, from the right-sized turf to the number of players in certain positions. Here are the game's essentials.

◉ THE PITCH ◉

Rugby's hallowed turf remains the same size the world over.

- A rugby pitch is 100 metres long and 70 metres wide.

- There are five crucial lines within this 100-metre space.

    1. **The try line:** the most important of them all, each try line is exactly 100 metres from the other. In the middle of this white line are the goal posts. Players must place the ball on or behind the line in order to score a try, or against the foot of the goal posts.
    2. **The 22-metre line:** found 22 metres out from the try lines. If a team touch the ball down in their own goal area, then they must restart the game with a drop kick from either on or behind the 22-metre line.
    3. **The 10-metre line:** situated either side of the half-way line, restarts after a try, penalty or drop goal from the half-way line must go a minimum 10 metres from the kick-off.
    4. **The half-way line:** 50 metres from the try lines, both sides kick off and restart the game following a try, drop goal or penalty from this point.
    5. **The touchline:** on either side of the pitch, the ball is out of play any time it passes over the touchline.

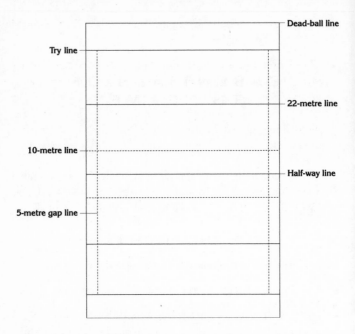

Layout of a rugby pitch

Pocket fact H
The only time a team keeps possession of the ball after kicking it into touch is when kicking into touch from a penalty.

Other lines on the pitch include the 5-metre line, the 15-metre line and the dead-ball line.

- **The 5-metre lines:** rugby uses two versions of the 5-metre line. The first is placed 5 metres out from the try line. A knock-on or forward pass between the 5-metre line and the try line results in a scrum on the 5-metre line. The second 5-metre line is placed 5 metres infield from the touchline and is used to create the gap between the hooker throwing in and the lineout.

- **The 15-metre line:** positioned 15 metres infield from the touchline. Any offences at the lineout that are sanctioned by the referee result in a scrum on the 15-metre line, in line with where the lineout was taken. Also, players who are not involved in a lineout are not allowed to advance until the ball has left the area between the 15-metre line and the 5-metre line.

- **The dead-ball line:** situated outside the 100-metre length of the pitch, there is a 22-metre gap between the try line and the dead-ball line. If the ball passes this line and goes 'dead', then the defending team has the option of a 22 dropout or a scrum from where the ball was kicked dead.

Using these lines, certain areas of the pitch become defined.

- **The 22:** the area between the try line and the 22-metre line, the majority of points in a match arguably come from this part of the field, with penalties, drop goals and tries easier to make the nearer the player is to the try line and goal posts. As a result of this, cynical play by the defending team such as slowing the ball down at the breakdown or offsides in this area will be punished more severely by the referee.

- **The in-goal area:** the area between the try line and dead-ball line, this is the area where tries are scored. The length of this area is a maximum of 22 metres, but the actual size varies depending on the size of the pitch or stadium, with most international stadiums having bigger in-goal areas than those at club level.

Pocket fact H

The smallest size for an in-goal area is 10 metres, at the Madejski Stadium in Reading, which is the home of London Irish, while the one at Twickenham is the maximum 22. All areas must be 70 metres wide.

☉ THE GOALPOSTS ☉

Rugby goals are formed from two high white posts and one crossbar. The two white posts are positioned 5.6 metres apart, with a 3-metre high crossbar. The two posts themselves must be taller than the minimum of 3.4 metres, and their size varies from domestic level to international level.

Pocket fact H

The first goalposts were introduced at Rugby School during the 1830s. They have always been painted white.

☉ POSITIONS ☉

Set positions on the rugby field have developed over time with the additions of the scrum and lineout to the sport. Divided into forwards and backs a fair amount of banter and camaraderie has built up between the two sections of players.

The structure of a rugby side generally looks like this.

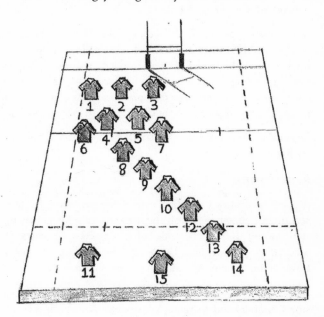

1 AND 3: PROPS

The really big men up front, the prop's jobs are to ensure that the scrum does not collapse, and to lift the second rows in the line-out. In a sense the fate of any scrum rests on the prop's broad shoulders, with the opportunity to win penalties, free kicks, or a scrum for their side if they are able to better their opponent in the engagement.

Working with the hooker in the centre, there are two types of prop; a loosehead and a tighthead. When setting in the scrum each player aims to place their head in the space to the left of their opposite man. Forcing an opponent to drop his bind, or collapse the scrum due to being unable to handle the power of the opposite man, can not only create the opportunity for points but also bragging rights over the opposite man. It is as much about strength as it is about technique.

In the lineout, props will often stand either side of the player who is set to be lifted to contest the ball. They will move up and down the line depending on where the jumper is positioned, before lifting and holding the man up in the air for as long as possible until either the ball is secured, or the opportunity has gone. Props must ensure that the man is brought down safely to avoid serious injury.

Legends: Jason Leonard (England), Fran Cotton (England), Os du Randt (South Africa).

2: HOOKER

Arguably the most important man at the set piece. A successful scrum and lineout relies on the hooker doing his job with constant success. In the scrum his task is to retrieve the ball after the scrum-half puts it into the tunnel by hooking it backwards towards the number 8, hence the name of 'hooker'.

In the lineout, the hooker throws the ball in, aiming to hit on his side's jumpers and to retain possession. With both scrums and lineouts being vital when attacking the try line or desperately defending near their own line, the hooker's job is of great importance. A good throw could win a match, whilst a miss in the last minute could cost his side the game.

Legends: Sean Fitzpatrick (New Zealand), Brian Moore (England), Keith Wood (Ireland).

Pocket fact H

John Smit became the first hooker to lift the World Cup trophy when he captained South Africa to victory in France 2007.

4 AND 5: SECOND ROWS

The engine-room of the side, second rows are normally the tallest players on the field. They form the central part of the scrum, lining up behind the front row of the two props and hooker, and in front of the back row of flankers and the number 8. Some of the game's most physically imposing figures have been second rows, with their height advantage enabling them to make some devastating tackles.

Second rows are also crucial in the lineout. They are lifted into the air by the props in order to win the ball thrown in by the hooker, but must do so whilst beating the opposition's jumpers to the ball. It's a position that requires more than just muscle and weight but great athleticism and agility as well.

Legends: Willie John McBride (Ireland), Colin Meads (New Zealand), John Eales (Australia), Martin Johnson (England).

6 AND 7: FLANKERS

Arguably the hardest working players on the pitch, flankers are tasked with making the biggest tackles and securing the ball at the ruck area. Masters of the dark arts of the breakdown, flankers normally secure more balls than any other player at the ruck area as it is their job to get to the rucks first to either secure the ball or try and steal it from their opponent.

There are two types of flanker, the blindside and the openside. The blindside flanker wears number 6 and is positioned on the blind side of the play with the scrum between him and the rest of the pitch, while the openside flanker wears number 7 and is on the side of the scrum open to the play.

Their positioning on the sides of the scrum enables them to break off quicker in order to play a crucial part in either the first phase attack or to make the first tackle. Given that they tend to play on the edge, they also come with a reputation for pushing the boundaries of the rulebook, and are frequently penalised at the tackle area.

Legends: Michael Jones (New Zealand), Fergus Slattery (Ireland), Francois Pienaar (South Africa), Richie McCaw (New Zealand).

8: NUMBER 8

Traditionally the big man at the back of the scrum, number 8s are renowned for their dynamic running off the back of the scrum and in open play. Over the years the role has developed, with number 8s in attack often being used as a third centre as the levels of physicality have increased. They are often the quickest members of the forward pack.

At the scrum it is the number 8's responsibility to ensure the ball is secure for either himself to pick up and run with it, or to make it comfortably available for his scrum-half. In the lineout, number 8s are often used as jumpers due to their athleticism, as a minor third option in order to confuse the opposition defence.

Legends: Lawrence Dallaglio (England), Morne du Plessis (South Africa), Zinzan Brooke (New Zealand).

Pocket fact H

The number 8 position was created in 1928 by South African Oubaas Markötter to make use of a back called André Macdonald, who was allegedly too slow to be a back and too small to be a forward. His positioning at the back of the scrum, and his interaction with the scrum-half, were innovative.

9: SCRUM-HALF

Along with the fly-half, scrum-halves form the heartbeat of any rugby team. Their positioning between the forward pack and the rest of the back line makes them crucial in attack. They are the primary source in terms of distribution and are the starting point for any passages of play in the backs.

At the set-piece, scrum-halves receive the ball from either the top of the lineout or at the back of the scrum. In addition, at the scrum it is the scrum-half's job to put the ball into the gap between the two packs of forwards.

Common traits found in scrum-halves include excellent pace and handling of the ball, but also leadership skills. Acting as a bridge between the forwards and the backs, the scrum-half can constantly be heard directing, or berating, his teammates.

Legends: Nick Farr-Jones (Australia), Gareth Edwards (Wales), Agustin Pichot (Argentina), Joost van der Westhuizen (South Africa), George Gregan (Australia).

10: FLY-HALF

The glory position. Fly-halves are responsible for directing a side both in attack and in defence. If a game is tight at the death, and a team is searching for a moment of inspiration, then it is the fly-half who tends to step forward.

Attacking-wise, fly-halves can pick from three options once they have possession: pass, kick or run. A position that requires excellent handling as well as an accurate boot, they dictate the pace of the attack. A fly-half's kicking is as important in gaining beneficial field position and scoring penalties and drop goals, as it is when desperately defending. Lastly, a fly-half with genuine pace can outwit opposition defences by running through the narrowest of gaps when the opposition are trying to predict what they will do next.

Legends: Jonny Wilkinson (England), Grant Fox (New Zealand), Diego Dominguez (Italy), Neil Jenkins (Wales), Naas Botha (South Africa), Phil Bennett (Wales).

Pocket fact H

Some positions are referred to by different names in other regions. The fly-half position is often referred to as the 'outside half' in the UK, while in Ireland it is sometimes called the 'outhalf' position. In New Zealand, the fly-half is often called the 'first five-eighth', with the centre outside him becoming the 'second five-eighth'.

11 AND 14: WINGERS

Wingers in the modern game come in all shapes and sizes, but with the same raw ability, pace and natural instinct, making them masters of the art of finishing tries.

Positioned on the right and left sides of the pitch, wingers are also important in defence as they can often be left in one-on-one positions with the opposition running at them. They will also track back when it appears as though the opposition are preparing to kick the ball downfield, either to prevent the ball from going into touch or to start a counter-attack.

Legends: Jonah Lomu (New Zealand), David Campese (Australia), Gerald Davies (Wales), Tony O'Reilly (Ireland), Rory Underwood (England).

12 AND 13: CENTRES

The two men in the middle. A position that has evolved dramatically over the last 20 years in terms of physicality, there are two types of centre, inside and outside.

Inside centres tend to be similar to fly-halves, with good hands and an astute kicking game. Outside centres are among the fastest players in the side and must be excellent at searching for gaps in the defence, and in timing their runs off the fly-half. Offloading in the tackle is also another big part of a modern centre's game.

For both centres, their defence must also be exceptional, given that the majority of attacks pass through the area where they are located. Centres are often the key defensive organisers for their side, so communication skills and high levels of fitness are important.

Legends: Brian O'Driscoll (Ireland), Philippe Sella (France), Danie Gerber (South Africa), Mike Gibson (Ireland).

Pocket fact H

The highest ever try scorer at international level is winger Daisuke Ohata of Japan. Ohata was capped 58 times by the Japanese national side, scoring 69 tries from his debut against Wales in November 1996 until his retirement in January 2011.

15: FULL-BACK

The last line of defence, a full-back will position himself behind his side's defensive line to protect the try line if the opposition break through. This positioning further back down the pitch is also important for the fielding of opposition kicks, and full-backs are often responsible(along with the fly-half), for clearing the ball away when under pressure in defence.

The position requires a good measure of bravery as well as strong handling skills. Often the target for 'up and unders' (see Glossary, p.180) from the opposition, full-backs must be aware of where the ball is set to land and also time their run to perfection in order to beat the opposition to the high ball.

As well as important defensive duties, full-backs are often the creators of many brilliant counter-attacks. From their deep position, they can spot where the space might be to launch a break, or any potential mismatches between quicker players like wingers and centres against slower ones like props or hookers.

Legends: Serge Blanco (France), Gavin Hastings (Scotland), J P R Williams (Wales), Percy Montgomery (South Africa).

☺ REFEREEING ☺

Rugby's man in the middle commands more respect than his footballing counterpart. Stemming from the age of referees as schoolmasters, the referee is politely and respectfully addressed as 'sir' during the match, and is never surrounded by a mob of protesting players as is often seen in football.

HISTORY

After rugby's inception in the 1800s, in its primary years the game was played without any referees at all. The game was run by the team's two captains, who would call offences when they spotted them and come to an agreement over the decision. The advantage law was born out of this arrangement, because captains would not attempt to stop the game if they felt that their team had an advantage in attack.

Following the creation of the IRB, the laws of the game were changed so that every match required a referee and two touch judges to be present. This automatically led to better officiating of the game, preventing repeats of the controversial results that had happened in the past. Today's game features the same number of refereeing officials on the field, except since the turn of the last century they have been given earpieces and microphones in order to communicate with each other on the field. This means that decisions from the touch judges can be called while play is still carrying on, instead of having to wait for a break.

ROLE OF THE REFEREE

It sounds basic, but the role of the referee is quite simply to make sure that the game runs smoothly and safely and to punish any indiscretions.

Whatever advice he may receive from the other officials on and off the field, it is the referee who calls the shots. Here are his primary concerns.

Safety

With its lack of padding and protection, rugby is one of the more dangerous sports in the world. Numerous incidents in the game's history, including 71 recorded fatalities, have led to the governing bodies attempting to make the game safer in order to prevent future tragedies on the field.

During the match, it is the referee's responsibility to make sure that any severe incidents are either prevented or properly punished. For example, if at any moment during the preparation for a scrum the referee is unhappy with either side, or the shape of the scrum as both teams prepare to 'crouch, touch, pause and engage', then he will stop the game and reset the scrum. This may lead to displeasure and booing from the crowd, but is essential to prevent any accidents.

Again, during open play, if a player appears to be either concussed or knocked out following a collision, the referee must attempt to stop the game as quickly as possible so that the player can be treated. If a player is seriously injured following a dangerous or late tackle from an opponent, then the appropriate disciplinary action must be carried out, with the referee able to issue yellow or red cards depending on the severity of the incident (see p.34).

Letting the game flow

Nothing is worse than watching a game of rugby which is constantly stopping and starting. Therefore, whilst obviously needing to maintain the letter of the law, to keep the match a spectacle it is also crucial for the referee to keep the game moving by playing the 'advantage' law when possible, particularly with regard to small infringements such as knock-ons.

Discipline

Whilst referees will try to play advantage when possible, there are some incidents that require instant action. For serial offences such as killing the ball at the ruck, late tackles and offsides, teams will normally be given a series of warnings not to infringe again. Depending on the referee's degree of leniency or strictness, if the team continues to commit the same offences, then he will have no option but to issue a yellow card to the offending player.

However, for more serious offences such as stamping, gouging, fighting and dangerous tackles, referees have been known to issue straight red cards without any prior warning. Red cards are still rare in rugby, as referees prefer to keep the game a contest for as long as possible. Any severe incidents must then be reported after the final whistle to the governing body that organised the match, so an appropriate punishment can be decided.

Pocket fact H

Over 110 players have received red cards at international level. No one has ever received two.

OTHER OFFICIALS

The touch judges

Gone are the days when touch judges were simply involved in order to mark where the ball left the field of play. In the modern game, the men on the sidelines are often brought in for consultation by the referee, and are also able to recommend punishments for anything they might have seen during a passage of play that the referee has missed, including off the ball incidents between players or any knock-ons or forward passes that have gone unnoticed.

Touch judges communicate with the referee via headsets, and will also wave their flags during the passage of play if they notice an offence. At the next stoppage the referee will then consult the touch judge who will recommend a suitable action for the referee. Touch judges can also be consulted regarding the awarding of a try, if they have a better angle when viewing the grounding of the ball.

When the ball leaves the field of play, the touch judge will raise his flag from the mark where the ball has gone out, and then with his other arm motion towards the side of the team who will then take the resulting lineout.

For penalty kicks and conversion attempts, both touch judges are required to stand behind the posts and judge whether the ball has gone through. If the kick is successful, then they will raise their flags to indicate to the referee and the crowd that the points have been awarded to the attacking side. If it is unsuccessful, then their flags stay down.

The fourth official

Similar to the role of the fourth official used in Association Football, the other man on the sideline is in charge of substitutions. They will indicate to the referee the shirt number of the players coming off and going on. They are also used as a back-up touch judge if one of the original officials picks up an injury.

Television match official

The final member of the officiating team, the Television Match Official, or TMO as it is also known. The TMO is used by the referee on occasions when he is unsure about the grounding of a try. The TMO can use slow motion replays from various angles to help determine whether a try has been legitimately scored or not.

When addressed by a referee, they will have to answer one of two questions, depending on the level of uncertainty in the referee's mind.

- 'Is there any reason why I cannot award the try?'
- 'Try or no try?'

A TMO might not award the try for a number of reasons, for example because the ball is held up, or has been knocked on, or because the player has not placed enough downward pressure on the ball with the hands or arms.

There are times when the TMO may simply not be able to see whether the ball has been scored due to the views from various camera angles being obscured by bodies, for example for attempted tries around the ruck area or following a maul. In this case, it is impossible for the try to be given by the TMO so the benefit of the doubt is given to the defending team.

An infamous TMO decision

During the 2007 World Cup final in Paris, the use of the TMO left its mark on rugby history, but for the wrong reason. When Mark Cueto went over in the left corner following a good break from Mathew Tait, England looked to be back in the match with the score potentially 8–9 and a conversion to come. Referee Alain Rolland wanted to make sure of the grounding, given the importance of the occasion and because Cueto's legs were near the touchline, he referred the incident to TMO Stuart Dickinson.

The consequent replays indicated that the try was good, as Cueto had grounded the ball correctly and his legs had not gone into touch until after the ball had been placed over the line. However, with the crowd and players convinced, Dickinson then looked at the replays several more times before deciding that Cueto's legs were out in touch, meaning the try was disallowed, with the score remaining at 3–9. South Africa went on to win the final, and their second World Cup, by 15–6.

4

OTHER FORMS OF
THE GAME

The split between rugby league and rugby union has created two great forms of the game, which please fans all over the world. There's also a growing following for other forms of the game, though, including sevens, tag or touch rugby, and the women's game has also seen a rise in popularity over the last few years. This chapter looks at these other forms of the game.

◉ DIFFERENCES BETWEEN ◉
LEAGUE AND UNION

Since the gradual split between the two sports in 1895, the two types of rugby have gone in very different directions. Here are the vital differences.

- Rugby league teams have 13 players as opposed to 15 in rugby union.

- League pitches are a maximum 122 metres, whilst union pitches are 144 metres.

- League uses a six tackle rule. After six tackles the team in possession must hand over the ball to the opposition. The ball cannot be contested after the player is tackled as in rugby union, with the opposition having to let the player in possession get to his feet and recycle the ball.

- A try is worth four points in league as opposed to five points in union.

- Penalty goals and drop goals are worth one and two points respectively in league, as opposed to three points apiece in union.

SCRUMS

A lot of key parts of rugby union have gradually been phased out of rugby league, mainly the areas of restarting the game. Lineouts do not exist; instead, when the ball goes out of play, the opposition uses a scrum in order to restart the match. These scrums are 20 metres infield from the point where the ball has gone out. However, if the ball goes straight out into touch from the kick, then the opposition wins a scrum from the point where the ball was kicked.

Scrums in rugby league are not competitive. They take place mainly as a means to restart the match, with neither team pushing against each other in the scrum, instead simply resting against each other in a scrum formation.

KICKING

Kicking in rugby league is also different from rugby union. On the fifth tackle, league players will often try and use grubber kicks, up and unders and banana kicks (see Glossary) in order to score tries or retrieve possession. Tactical kicking like that found in rugby union is uncommon in rugby league, where the emphasis is on trying to retain possession rather than gain significant field positions.

Pocket fact H

An up and under kick is sometimes referred to as a Garryowen, named after Garryowen RFC in Limerick, where they favour the high kick in the face of oncoming defenders.

DIFFERENT USES OF PLAYERS

Rugby league uses no flankers, reducing the numbers to 13. Players are also numbered differently. The order of numbers is in a sense reversed, with full-backs wearing the number 1 shirt through to the scrum-halves wearing number 7. In the forwards, props wear 8 and 10 with the hooker in the middle wearing number 9. Second row forwards are numbers 11 and 12. The rugby league equivalent of a number 8 is called a loose forward, and wears the number 13 shirt.

Given that the scrums are uncontested, there is no requirement for props and hookers to be as muscular and strong as they are in rugby union. As a result, forwards and backs are more physically similar to those in rugby union, creating an even level of athleticism and taking out any of the size or speed advantages sometimes found in rugby union. This means the game is arguably faster and more entertaining.

Other players who have set responsibilities in rugby union are not as important in rugby league. For example, second rows are essential to a fully functioning lineout and for pushing in the scrum in rugby union, hence their significant height and stature, but as there are no lineouts or contested scrums in league, these aspects of the position are not a crucial feature. The same can be said for the scrum-half, normally at the centre of the rucks and breakdown in rugby union, while in league anyone can fill the scrum-half role at the end of any tackle.

Pocket fact H

The first Rugby League World Cup was held in 1954 in France, featuring Great Britain, New Zealand, Australia and the host nation. It was won by Great Britain, who were captained by Huddersfield's David Valentine.

☻ RUGBY SEVENS ☻

Now a recognised Olympic sport, sevens has emerged as a major force on the international sporting stage. From its beginnings in Melrose, Scotland, back in the 1880s, the game has spread around the world, from Brazil to the Pacific Island nations of Fiji, Samoa and Tonga. Given its abbreviated form, sevens is arguably easier for new teams and nations to pick up, hence the spread of its popularity.

RULES

The abbreviated form of the game uses some variations on the original 15-man code.

- Each side plays with seven players, rather than 15.

- Halves are seven minutes each way.

- Scrums use three players instead of eight.

- Half-time lasts for one minute, and two minutes in finals.

- All conversions are taken with drop-kicks rather than using kicking tees.

- The team which has scored takes the kick-off to restart the game.

- Yellow cards lead to a suspension of two minutes rather than 10.

WORLD CUP SEVENS

As well as the annual World Cup Series, there is a World Cup Sevens tournament, held every four years since 1993. The first winners were England who narrowly beat Australia in the final of the tournament held in Scotland. Fiji are currently the most successful side, with two wins.

The current holders are Wales, who were outsiders for the 2009 tournament. They then stunned tournament favourites New Zealand by just a single point in the quarter-finals, before defeating Samoa and then Argentina on their way to victory. The next tournament will be held in 2013 in Russia.

SEVENS AT THE 2016 OLYMPIC GAMES

Rugby sevens was recommended for inclusion in the 2016 Olympics by the IOC executive committee in 2009 following an impressive application which included big-name ambassadors Lawrence Dallaglio, Jonah Lomu and sevens legend Waisale Serevi. The tournament in Rio de Janeiro will be the abbreviated game's first appearance at the Olympics. Twelve teams are expected to take part in both men's and women's competitions, with the hope that more teams can be included in the Olympics in 2020.

Pocket fact H

The USA are the most successful Olympic rugby team, having won gold medals in 1920 and 1924.

⬭ TOUCH AND TAG RUGBY ⬭

A variation on the original game, touch or tag rugby is a non-contact form of rugby, with players only having to touch the man with the ball using their hands in order to stop him, or in the case of tag rugby, to rip off a Velcro tag attached to the player's shorts. Once touched or tagged (sometimes an issue that is hotly contested) the player must pass the ball to another teammate. Similar to rugby league, each side gets six touches/tags before having to hand the ball over to the opposition if they haven't been able to score a try. Kicking is prohibited, with the emphasis on good hands and running lines.

⬭ MINI RUGBY ⬭

Every player has to start somewhere and for the majority of the game's global stars it begins in the minis. It is usually for players aged under 13 and there are over 3,000 rugby clubs in the UK, the majority of which have junior sections for mini rugby players.

There are three set stages of mini rugby.

- **Stage 1: mini tag rugby (U7 and U8)**

    For safety reasons, younger players are prevented from tackling one another. Instead, players have cloth strips attached to them by Velcro, and when the strip is pulled off the player is 'tackled', meaning the player has to pass the ball.

    Many of the main game's aspects such as rucking, mauling, tackling, lineouts and scrums are not used and there is no form of kicking. There are no conversions after tries either, meaning the only way to score points is by scoring tries. Teams are also much smaller in number, ranging from five to seven players.

● **Stage 2: mini rugby (U9 and U10)**

In the next stage, players are only prohibited from kicking and carrying out hand-offs. Scrums and lineouts are created using three players, though there is no lifting in the lineout. These are uncontested at U9 level, meaning the players do not jump for the opposition's ball. Teams now play 15-minute halves and use up to nine players per side.

Pocket fact H

Ten pairs of fathers and sons have played rugby for South Africa.

● **Stage 3: midi rugby (U11 and U12)**

With an increase in size of both the pitch and the ball, midi rugby sees young players step up a notch. Halves increase from 15 minutes to 20 minutes, and teams are now up to 12 or 13 players. Teams can take conversions after scoring tries, but other kicking such as drop goals and penalty goals is still not allowed.

Clubs up to U13 level put out mixed teams of boys and girls. With the reduced levels of intensity in terms of tackling and encouragement on passing and running, the game is more even at this age group with neither sex holding a significant physical advantage. From U13 level upwards, however, only same-sex teams are used.

The general theory is that players who start learning to train and play from a young age become better players over time. The majority of the game's leading international stars have all come through mini rugby ranks at their respective clubs around the world.

⊖ WOMEN'S RUGBY ⊖

The growth of the women's game around the world over the past couple of decades has been both swift and impressive. The game's rapid progressions have come from a growing awareness of the game and the introduction of professionalism, with more media attention focused on the women's game through the Six Nations tournaments and Women's Rugby World Cup.

HISTORY

For decades, women's rugby was a game played in secrecy, and as a result there is a lack of concrete information about its formative years. Various reports emerged from Ireland, England, New Zealand and France during the late 19th century and early 1900s of women's rugby being played, but it was done behind closed doors due to a large amount of public angst over the concept.

This trend continued during the 20th century, with the rare spectacle of public women's matches taking place between Cardiff and Newport Ladies at Cardiff Arms Park in 1917, during the First World War, and a game of rugby league in Australia between two women's teams in Sydney in 1921. Each time the games received negative public reactions, setting back the progress of the women's game.

It was not until the 1960s, with the creation of university rugby sides up and down the country, that women's rugby began to create a solid foundation, notably at Edinburgh University where the first recorded women's rugby team was founded in 1962. In a similar manner to the way men's rugby teams were created after schoolboys left their schools and moved into the working world, women's rugby teams started up following their departures from universities.

By the 1970s, the first national association had also been founded with the creation of the Association Francaise de Rugby Feminin (AFRF) in France. It would prove to be the catalyst for the formation of other clubs and unions around the world, including in Europe (Sweden, Spain, the Netherlands and Italy), as well as in Japan, Canada and the USA.

Pocket fact H

The first women's international match was held between the Netherlands and France in Utrecht in 1982, with the French winning 4–0.

The formation of the Women's Rugby Football Union (WRFU) in the UK in 1983 raised the game's status considerably. The majority of founding clubs were university teams from all over the country. Unions have since been formed in Italy, Canada and Japan, and national league and cup competitions have also been created.

As had been the case with the men's game nearly 100 years earlier, there was a need for a global governing organisation to oversee international regulation and competition. The WIRB was therefore created to fulfil a similar role as the IRB in the men's game. (See p.105 for more on women's rugby tournaments.)

Women's rugby clubs

In the Women's Premiership in England, half of the clubs share names, but not grounds, with clubs which have played in the men's Premiership, namely Bristol, London Wasps, Richmond, Saracens and Worcester. Other Women's Premiership sides, including Lichfield, Old Albanians and Darlington Mowden Park, have no equivalent men's team.

5

TEAM PROFILES

From the folklore banter of the amateur era to the glitzy modern professional game, rugby teams have been transformed in recent times, but the same sense of pride still remains. Here are the best club sides from around the world.

☉ THE ENGLISH (AVIVA) ☉ PREMIERSHIP

The principal domestic League in English rugby has been in existence since 1998, featuring 12 teams from across the country (see p.107 for more).

BATH

Ground: The Rec (Recreation Ground), Bath.

Honours: Six Premiership titles, 10 National Cups, one Heineken Cup (1998), one European Challenge Cup (2008).

Club legend: Jeremy Guscott – one of England's greatest centres, Guscott appeared 266 times for Bath during a 16-year stint at The Rec and was at the heart of Bath's glory days, including the Heineken Cup win in 1998.

Biggest win: Bath 84–Sale Sharks 7 (1997).

Biggest defeat: Bath 12–Gloucester 68 (2002).

Fan fact: No side has won more national cups than Bath, whose 10 titles all came in the 12 years between 1984 to 1996.

EXETER CHIEFS

Ground: Sandy Park, Exeter.

Honours: One Championship title (2010).

Club legend: Robert Baxter – a back row who put in 275 performances for Exeter, Baxter also went on to become head coach at the club, leading them to promotion at the end of the 2010 season. His brother, Richard, a number 8, holds the appearances record for the side with over 330 games.

Biggest win: Exeter 30–Northampton Saints 9 (2010).

Biggest defeat: Exeter 13–Harlequins 40 (2010).

Fan fact: Exeter moved to Sandy Park in 2006 from the County Ground, where they had played for over 100 years, including a match against the touring All Blacks in 1905.

GLOUCESTER

Ground: Kingsholm, Gloucester.

Honours: Four Premiership titles, seven National Cups, one European Challenge Cup, one Middlesex sevens title.

Club legend: Mike Teague – one of England's greatest back row internationals, Teague represented Gloucester 291 times, and holds the record for the most tries by a forward in a season with 21.

Biggest win: Gloucester 106–Bucharest Wolves 3 (2005).

Biggest defeat: Gloucester 19–Harlequins 75 (1996).

Fan fact: Gloucester have become synonymous with their kit colours, earning them the nickname 'Cherry & Whites'. Surprisingly though their first kit was all navy blue and their current kit is in fact based on the kit of local club Painswick RFC.

HARLEQUINS

Ground: The Stoop, Twickenham, London.

Honours: Two National Cups, three European Challenge Cups, one Championship title, one Powergen National Trophy, 14 Middlesex sevens titles.

Club legend: Adrian Stoop – after representing Harlequins 182 times between 1901 and 1939, Stoop was the club's president from 1920–1949. Harlequins ground is named after Stoop for his commitment to the club.

Biggest win: Harlequins 88–Thurrock 0 (2000).

Biggest defeat: Harlequins 19–Bath 77 (2000).

Fan fact: Harlequins share both their name and ground with Harlequins Rugby League, formerly known as the London Broncos, London Crusaders and Fulham. They played at The Stoop twice in the late 1990s, when they were the Broncos, and from 2006 to the present day as Harlequins RL.

LEICESTER TIGERS

Ground: Welford Road, Leicester.

Honours: Nine Premiership titles, six National Cups, two Heineken Cups, one Middlesex sevens title (1995).

Club legend: Dusty Hare – William Henry 'Dusty' Hare played for Leicester for 14 years up to 1989 and holds the world record for the most points scored in a first-class rugby career, with 7,337. He notched up 394 appearances at Leicester playing at full-back and was a firm favourite with the fans.

Biggest win: Leicester 100–Liverpool St Helens 0 (1992).

Biggest defeat: Leicester 10–The Barbarians 85 (2000).

Fan fact: Although incredibly successful on the rugby pitch, off it during the late 2000s a group of Leicester players including George Chuter, Aaron Mauger, Dan Hipkiss, Ayoola Erinle and Sam Vesty played in a band called Slo Progress, regularly gigging around Leicester and performing in aid of the Matt Hampson Foundation.

Pocket fact H

In 2005 England under-21 player Matt Hampson suffered a spinal injury during practice which left him paralysed. Following the accident, the Matt Hampson Foundation was formed in 2011 to raise funds and offer support for young people with similar injuries. Matt works at the foundation offering support and advice for those with similar injuries to his own.

LONDON IRISH

Ground: Madejski Stadium, Reading.

Honours: One National Cup (2002), one Middlesex sevens title (2009).

Club legend: Neal Hatley – now the club's forwards coach, Hatley made 193 Premiership appearances, 184 of them coming for London Irish at loosehead prop. His service to the game was rewarded when he captained the England Saxons side in the Churchill Cup, before retiring.

Biggest win: London Irish 62–Harlequins 14 (1998).

Biggest defeat: London Irish 16–Bath 64 (2000).

Fan fact: Irish's nickname of The Exiles originated in the club's formative years when it was established as the local London side for Irishmen based around the city. Over the years, however, the club has become a home for players from all over the world, not just Ireland, making the Exiles nickname all the more pertinent.

LONDON WASPS

Ground: Adams Park, High Wycombe.

Honours: Six Premiership titles, three National Cups, two Heineken Cups, one European Challenge Cup, five Middlesex sevens titles.

Club legend: Lawrence Dallaglio – often referred to as 'Mr Wasps', Dallaglio spent his entire playing career at Wasps, making 339 appearances. He was the inspirational captain who helped Wasps to multiple successes during the late 1990s and early 2000s, including five Premiership titles and two Heineken Cups.

Biggest win: London Wasps 71–West Hartlepool 14 (1998).

Biggest defeat: London Wasps 21–Newcastle Falcons 59 (2000).

Fan fact: In the 2007 Six Nations match between Wales and England in Cardiff, the entire English back row came from Wasps, with James Haskell, Joe Worsley and Tom Rees all playing. It was the first time any club had supplied the entire back row to the national team.

Pocket fact H

The popular rugby anthem Swing Low, Sweet Chariot, *a gospel hymn of African/American origin, has undergone numerous cover versions over time, notably every four years for the Rugby World Cup. China Black and Ladysmith Black Mambazo sold 200,000 copies of their version in 1995, while Russell Watson, UB40, Blake and O.L.M. have all released covers for the subsequent tournaments.*

NEWCASTLE FALCONS

Ground: Kingston Park, Newcastle.

Honours: One Premiership title (1998), one Championship title (1993), four National Cups, one Middlesex sevens title (2007).

Club legend: Jonny Wilkinson – during his 11 years at Newcastle he helped them to Premiership success in 1998 and two National Cups.

Biggest win: Newcastle Falcons 156–Rugby Lions 5 (1996).

Biggest defeat: Newcastle Falcons 10–Leicester Tigers 83 (2000).

Fan fact: After Sir John Hall invested in the club, Newcastle became the rugby world's first 'professional' club and Rob Andrew was employed as director of rugby on a salary.

NORTHAMPTON SAINTS

Ground: Franklin's Gardens, Northampton.

Honours: One Championship title (2008), one Heineken Cup (1999), one European Challenge Cup (2009), one EDF Energy Cup (2008), one Middlesex sevens title (2003).

Club legend: Ron Jacobs – he holds the record for the most appearances with 470 games. Jacobs was also a prominent England international during his 17-year career, including a stint captaining the side towards the end of his career. He was President of the RFU in the 1980s.

Biggest win: Northampton Saints 96–Sedgley Park 3 (2008).

Biggest defeat: Northampton Saints 12–London Wasps 54 (2000).

Fan fact: During their season in the Championship in 2008, Saints finished undefeated with 30 wins in 30 matches, notching up 143 points.

SALE SHARKS

Ground: Edgeley Park, Stockport.

Honours: One Premiership title (2005), two European Challenge Cups.

Club legend: Steve Hanley – spending a decade at the club between 1998 and 2008, Hanley remains the Premiership's all-time leading try scorer, with 75. In total he scored 104 in 191 matches for Sale, and one try for England in his only appearance for the national side.

Biggest win: Sale Sharks 97–E1 Salvador (2010).

Biggest defeat: Sale Sharks 0–Harlequins 49 (2007).

Fan fact: The first Sale player to represent the club at international level was G A M Isherwood on the 1910 Lions tour to South Africa.

SARACENS

Ground: Vicarage Road, Watford.

Honours: One Premiership title (2011), one National Cup (1998).

Club legend: Francois Pienaar – played with the winning South African national side in the 1995 World Cup and joined Saracens in 1996 as player/coach. He led them to cup glory in 1998, defeating London Wasps in the final.

Biggest win: Saracens 66–Leeds Carnegie 7 (2008).

Biggest defeat: Saracens 21–Bath 66 (2008).

Fan fact: Following a tour to Japan in 2002, Saracens developed a partnership with Japanese club side Fukuoka Sanix Blues, with players transferring between the two clubs in recent years.

Pocket fact H

Sean Connery, Bill Clinton, Che Guevara and Ted Kennedy all played rugby in their younger days.

WORCESTER WARRIORS

Ground: Sixways Stadium, Worcester.

Honours: Two Championship titles.

Club legend: Pat Sanderson – a talismanic figure at Sixways, Sanderson joined from Harlequins in 2004 and captained Worcester in the Premiership to great effect, as well as captaining England.

Biggest win: Worcester Warriors 81–Bristol 13 (2011).

Biggest defeat: Worcester Warriors 3–Sale Sharks 57 (2004).

Fan fact: Worcester reached the top flight for the first time in 2004 after winning a record 26 (out of 26) matches that season.

⊚ CELTIC LEAGUE ⊚

A tournament played between professional teams from Ireland, Italy, Scotland and Wales, the Celtic League was introduced to create higher levels of competition between the countries' domestic leagues and the Heineken Cup (see p.109 for more on this).

AIRONI RUGBY

Ground: Stadio Luigi Zaffanella.

Honours: None.

Club legend: Salvatore Perugini – given that Aironi have only been in existence for two seasons, there are not many obvious candidates. However, prop Perugini, who holds the bizarre record of being the player with the highest numbers of caps to never have scored any points with 83, joined the franchise after several years of success playing for Toulouse.

Biggest win: Aironi 32–Edinburgh 15 (2011).

Biggest defeat: Aironi 10–Scarlets 49 (2010).

Fan fact: Created in 2010 for inclusion into the Celtic League, Aironi was created out of eight Italian rugby clubs, with 54% of the new club coming from Rugby Viadana.

BENETTON TREVISO

Ground: Stadio Comunale di Monigo.

Honours: 15 Italian Super 10 titles, four Coppa Italias.

Club legend: Alessandro Troncon – one of the greatest scrum halves to play the game, Troncon had two stints playing for

Treviso, between 1995–1999 and 2002–2006. At national level, Troncon won 101 caps for Italy, more than 50 of those alongside Diego Dominguez.

Biggest win: Benetton Treviso 50–Newport Gwent Dragons 24 (2011).

Biggest defeat: Benetton Treviso 5–London Wasps 71 (2006).

Fan fact: Founded in 1932, Treviso did not win their first honour until 20 years later when they won their first Italian championship.

CARDIFF BLUES

Ground: Cardiff City Stadium.

Honours: One Anglo-Welsh Cup (2009), one European Challenge Cup (2010).

Club legend: Paul Tito – the man from Taumarunui, New Zealand, came to the Blues in 2007 and after receiving the captaincy the following year, led the Cardiff side to glory in both the Anglo-Welsh Cup and European competition.

Biggest win: Cardiff Blues 58–Connacht 0 (2008).

Biggest defeat: Cardiff Blues 3–Leeds 58 (2006).

Fan fact: Cardiff's victory over Toulon in the 2010 European Challenge Cup final was the first time a Welsh side had won a European trophy.

CONNACHT RUGBY

Ground: Galway Sportsground.

Honours: Two Irish Inter-Provinicial Championships.

Club legend: Ray McCoughlin – the British & Irish Lions prop won 40 caps for Ireland, as well as impressing on the Lions tours of 1971 and 1966.

Biggest win: Connacht 62–Caerphilly 0 (2001).

Biggest defeat: Connacht 0–Cardiff Blues 58 (2008).

Fan fact: The Galway Sportsground has a dog racing track around the outside of the pitch, which is often used after matches finish.

EDINBURGH RUGBY

Ground: Murrayfield Stadium, Edinburgh.

Honours: None.

Club legend: Chris Paterson – a mainstay of both the Edinburgh and Scottish national side over the last decade. Paterson's boot has proved to be exceptionally clinical, with his Edinburgh points record at the start of the season standing at 771.

Biggest win: Edinburgh Rugby 62–Connacht 13 (2009).

Biggest defeat: Edinburgh Rugby 0–Northampton Saints 37 (2010).

Fan fact: Edinburgh played in the first ever Inter-provincial match when they defeated Glasgow in 1872.

Pocket fact H

The total audience for the Rugby World Cup in 2007 was 4.2 billion over the 48 matches.

GLASGOW WARRIORS

Ground: Firhill Stadium, Glasgow.

Honours: None.

Club legend: Dan Parks – now at Cardiff Blues, Parks signed for Glasgow in 2003 and amassed nearly 1,700 points to become the league's leading scorer of all time.

Biggest win: Glasgow 59–Pontypridd 14 (2001).

Biggest defeat: Glasgow 19–Leicester Tigers 90 (1997).

Fan fact: Three sets of brothers have turned out for Glasgow since their inception: Alan and Gordon Bulloch, Thom and Max Evans, and Rory and Sean Lamont.

LEINSTER

Ground: RDS Arena and Aviva Stadium, Dublin.

Honours: Two Heineken Cups, two Celtic League titles, 22 Irish Inter-Provincial Championships.

Club legend: Brian O'Driscoll – the most talented centre of his generation, O'Driscoll has made more than 130 appearances for Leinster in over a decade, proving influential in their domestic and European success, as well as with Ireland and the British & Irish Lions.

Biggest win: Leinster 92–Bourgoin 17 (2004).

Biggest defeat: Leinster 20–Scarlets 51 (2004).

Fan fact: Although Leinster currently play in a navy-blue strip, the kit was originally green.

Pocket fact H

Leinster and Ireland prop Cian Healy is also an established DJ, playing under the moniker DJ Church, and has performed at many clubs and at the Oxygen music festival in Ireland.

MUNSTER

Ground: Thomond Park, Limerick, and Musgrave Park, Cork.

Honours: Two Heineken Cups, three Celtic League titles, one Celtic Cup, 22 Irish Inter-Provinicial Championships.

Club legend: Ronan O'Gara – now in his 15th season with Munster, O'Gara has been the influential fly-half and points scorer for the Irish side since 1997, leading them to multiple Celtic League and Heineken Cup trophies.

Biggest win: Munster 64–Viadana 0 (2002).

Biggest defeat: Munster 14–Cardiff Blues 60 (2004).

Fan fact: Munster have beaten many international touring sides in their time, including New Zealand, Australia and Morocco.

NEWPORT-GWENT DRAGONS

Ground: Rodney Parade, Newport.

Honours: None.

Club legend: Michael Owen – Wales Grand-Slam winning captain in 2005, Owen played for the Dragons from 2003–2008, during which he was selected for the British & Irish Lions tour for New Zealand. He made 98 appearances for the province, scoring 9 tries.

Biggest win: Dragons 48–Border Reivers 0 (2007).

Biggest defeat: Dragons 3–Leinster 55 (2005).

Fan fact: The Dragons best finish in the Celtic League came in their debut season in 2003, when they finished third.

OSPREYS

Ground: Liberty Stadium, Swansea.

Honours: Three Celtic League titles, one EDF Energy Cup (2008).

Club legend: Shane Williams – the Ospreys' top try scorer, Williams' magic has lit up Welsh rugby throughout his playing career. A winger, his trademark turn of pace resulted in several memorable scores.

Biggest win: Ospreys 68–Benetton Treviso 8 (2008).

Biggest defeat: Ospreys 6–Cardiff Blues 43 (2003).

Fan fact: For the 2008 match between Wales and England, the Ospreys provided 13 of the Welsh starting line-up, a Six Nations record.

SCARLETS

Ground: Parc y Scarlets, Llanelli.

Honours: one Celtic League title (2004).

Club legend: Simon Easterby – the current defence coach, Easterby has been at the Scarlets since 1999 and captained the side for five seasons during the 2000s.

Biggest win: Llanelli Scarlets 127–Slovenia 7 (2002).

Biggest defeat: Llanelli Scarlets 3–New Zealand 81 (1997).

Fan fact: In 2008, the Scarlets left their original home of Stradey Park in Llanelli where they had been based since 1879, a remarkable 129-year tenure. The last game played at Stradey was between the Scarlets and Bristol, with the home side comfortably winning 28–0.

ULSTER

Ground: Ravenhill, Belfast.

Honours: One Heineken Cup (1999), one Celtic League title (2006), one Celtic Cup (2003), 26 Irish Inter-Provincial titles.

Club legend: David Humphreys – the source of Ulster's success in the trophy cabinet, Humphreys captained the side to Heineken Cup glory in 1999 and kicked the winning drop goal against the Ospreys in the 2006 Celtic League final.

Biggest win: Ulster 59–Benetton Treviso 3 (2002).

Biggest defeat: Ulster 3–London Wasps 56 (1997).

Fan fact: Ulster were the only side to defeat the 1985/6 touring Australians, a feat that England, Scotland, Wales and Ireland failed to achieve.

⊖ FRENCH NATIONAL ⊖
RUGBY LEAGUE

The oldest league in rugby history, the following clubs are currently the biggest in the French Top 14, with varying levels of past success.

ASM CLERMONT AUVERGNE

Ground: Parc des Sports Marcel Michelin, Clermont-Ferrand.

Honours: One French Championship title, three Challenge Yves du Manoir Cups, one Coupe de France, two European Challenge Cups.

Club legend: Aurélien Rougerie – having joined the club when he was just six years old, Rougerie captained Clermont to their French Championship win in 2010.

Biggest win: Clermont 127–Racing CF 3 (2000).

Biggest defeat: Clermont 3–Toulon 58 (1992).

Fan fact: It took Clermont Auvergne 11 attempts to win their first Championship, having lost 10 previous finals until their success over Perpignan in 2010, the club's centenary year.

Pocket fact H

Gaston Vareilles was set to make his international debut for France against Scotland in 1910, but never did, due to a sandwich. During a brief stop at Lyon station, a hungry Vareilles got off to grab a bite to eat, but by the time he had finally got his sandwich, the train had left. He was never picked for France again.

RACING MÉTRO 92

Ground: Stade Olympique Yves-Du-Manoir, Paris.

Honours: Five French Championship titles, one Challenge Yves du Manoir Cup, two Rugby Pro D2 titles.

Club legend: Yves du Manoir – eternally remembered through the naming of Racing's stadium, du Manoir was a flamboyant fly-half adored by the crowds in the 1920s who tragically died in a plane crash aged 23.

Biggest win: Racing Métro 92 77–Venezia Mestre Rugby 6 (2008).

Biggest defeat: Racing Métro 92 3–Montauban 53 (2005).

Fan fact: The current club was formed from the two clubs Racing Club de Paris and US Métro in 2001. The 92 refers to the number of the Hauts-de-Seine department in the suburbs of Paris whose council gives financial backing.

RC TOULONNAIS

Ground: Stade Mayol, Toulon.

Honours: Three French Championship titles, two Challenge Yves du Manoir Cups, two Rugby Pro D2 titles.

Club legend: Éric Champ – a former president of the club, number 8 Champ spent his entire career at Toulon from 1979 to 1994, winning two French Championships. He also won 42 caps for France, scoring three tries.

Biggest win: Toulon 73–Rugby Rovigo 3 (2009).

Biggest defeat: Toulon 3–Gloucester 74 (2005).

Fan fact: Current owner Mourad Boudjellal, born and raised in Toulon, made his millions from the comic-strip industry.

STADE FRANÇAIS

Ground: Stade Charlety or Stade du France, Paris.

Honours: 13 French Championships, one Coupe de France.

Club legend: Christophe Dominici – the former France winger played for Stade for over a decade. Joining the club during their successful era in the early 2000s, he won five Championships on the left wing.

Biggest win: Stade Français 103–Racing CF 15 (2001).

Biggest defeat: Stade Français 3–La Rochelle 47 (2003).

Fan fact: Stade's players have become popular off the rugby field for the annual *Dieux de Stade* (Gods of Stade, or the Stadium) calendar. It pays homage to Greco-Roman athletes and the players are naked in the photos.

STADE TOULOUSAIN

Ground: Stade Ernest-Wallon and Stade Municipal de Toulouse, Toulouse.

Honours: Four Heineken Cup titles, 18 French Championship titles, three Coupe de France, five Challenge Yves du Manoir Cups.

Club legend: Guy Novès – a player in the 1980s, Novès has been the mastermind behind all of Toulouse success in the last 20 years since his return in 1993. Under his reign as head coach Toulouse have won four Heineken Cups and nine French Championships.

Biggest win: Stade Toulousain 108–Ebbw Vale 16 (1999).

Biggest defeat: Stade Toulousain 19–Bourgoin 82 (2003).

Fan fact: The club was founded in 1907 following an agreement between the previously feuding rugby teams from the town's university and veterinary school.

USA PERPIGNAN

Ground: Stade Aimé Grail.

Honours: Seven French Championship titles, three Challenge Yves du Manoir Cups.

Club legend: Nicolas Mas – the stalwart prop is the epitome of the Catalan region's passion, having captained and fought at the front of the scrum for over a decade during the 2000s.

Biggest win: USAP 98–Istres 14 (2001).

Biggest defeat: USAP 3–Newcastle 60 (1998).

Fan fact: In recognition of a fierce pride in their heritage, the club's colours are the Catalan red and gold, and the name, USAP, stands for *Unió e Sportiva Arlequins de Perpinyà* in Catalan.

⊜ SUPER RUGBY ⊜

Created following the dawn of professionalism in 1995, Super Rugby is a provincial tournament pitting teams from Australia, South Africa and New Zealand in one league (see p.115 for more).

AUCKLAND BLUES

Ground: Eden Park, Auckland, New Zealand.

Honours: Three Super Rugby titles.

Club legend: Carlos Spencer – nicknamed 'the king' and 'the magician', Spencer was a Super Rugby winner in 1996, 1997 and 2003 and racked up 96 appearances for the Blues in 11 years.

Biggest win: Blues 60–Hurricanes 7 (2001).

Biggest defeat: Blues 13–Queensland Reds 51 (1996).

Fan fact: Despite not reaching a final since 2003, the Blues remain the second most successful Super Rugby side ever, with three titles and one runners-up spot.

BLUE BULLS

Ground: Loftus Versfeld, Pretoria, South Africa.

Honours: Three Super Rugby titles, 23 Currie Cups (four shared), three Vodacom Cups.

Club legend: Frik du Preez – a true rugby superstar, du Preez played 109 times for Northern Transvaal from 1958 to 1971. A second row or flanker, he was an all-round rugby player, with remarkable pace and great athleticism in the lineout. He was also a renowned penalty and drop goal kicker, a rarity for a forward.

Biggest win: Bulls 92–Queensland Reds 3 (2007).

Biggest defeat: Bulls 3–ACT Brumbies 73 (1999).

Fan fact: Formerly known as Northern Transvaal, the club split from the Transvaal Rugby Football Union in 1938 and were renamed as the Blue Bulls in 1997.

ACT BRUMBIES

Ground: Canberra Stadium, Canberra, Australia.

Honours: Two Super Rugby titles.

Club legend: George Gregan – a mainstay of the Australian national side during the 1990s and 2000s, Gregan holds the Brumbies record for the most appearances, with 136.

Biggest win: Brumbies 64–Cats 0 (2001).

Biggest defeat: Brumbies 7–Hurricanes 56 (2009).

Fan fact: The Brumbies are the most successful Australian side in Super Rugby, having made five finals and won two championships.

CANTERBURY CRUSADERS

Ground: AMI Stadium, Christchurch, New Zealand .

Honours: Seven Super Rugby titles.

Club legend: Reuben Thorne – captain of the Crusaders and the All Blacks, Thorne won multiple titles playing in the back row during the 2000s.

Biggest win: Crusaders 96–NSW Waratahs 19 (2002).

Biggest defeat: Crusaders 16–Queensland Reds 52 (1996).

Fan fact: The Crusaders are the most successful Super Rugby side of all time with seven titles. The squad is made up of players from the Buller, Canterbury, Mid-Canterbury, South Canterbury, Tasman and West Coast ITM Cup teams.

Pocket fact H

New Zealand twins Alan and Gary Whetton, born 15 December 1959, both played every match in the 1987 Rugby World Cup, earning winners' medals at their home ground of Eden Park. They are the only set of twins ever to play together for the All Blacks.

QUEENSLAND REDS

Ground: Suncorp Stadium, Brisbane, Australia.

Honours: One Super Rugby title.

Club legend: Chris Latham – the Reds record try scorer with 38, over a decade Latham was one of the best full-backs in the world for Queensland. He finished his time with the Reds on 99 appearances.

Biggest win: Queensland Reds 53–Melbourne Rebels 3 (2011).

Biggest defeat: Queensland Reds 3–Blue Bulls 92 (2007).

Fan fact: From finishing 13th in 2009 to winning the competition just two years later in 2011, the Reds achieved a remarkable turnaround thanks to the work of new coach and former Wallaby World Cup winner Ewen McKenzie.

⊙ INTERNATIONAL TEAMS ⊙

There is no argument among players and fans that international rugby represents the highest and most difficult level of the game. A legend does not achieve such iconic status without having played a significant number of matches at test match level.

Here are the 10 foremost teams in world rugby, which have all featured for substantial periods of time in the top 10 of the IRB's world rankings.

ENGLAND

Founded: 1871.

Ground: Twickenham Stadium, Twickenham, London.

Honours: One World Cup, 26 Home Nations Championships (12 Grand Slams).

Greatest coach: Sir Clive Woodward, 1997–2004 – the only coach to lead England to World Cup glory, England also won three Six Nations championships under Woodward's tenure, including a Grand Slam in 2003.

Greatest player: Martin Johnson – England's captain during the late 1990s and early 2000s, he led the team to win the 2003 World Cup in Sydney.

Biggest win: England 134–Romania 0 (2001).

Biggest defeat: England 0–Australia 78 (1998).

Fan fact: The popular song *Swing Low, Sweet Chariot* has been heard around Twickenham since 1988, but sadly a rap version of the song featuring Jeremy Guscott was never released.

IRELAND

Founded: 1874.

Ground: Aviva Stadium, Dublin.

Honours: 11 Home Nations Championships (two Grand Slams).

Greatest coach: Declan Kidney – after winning two Heineken Cups with Munster, Kidney took the top job with Ireland and led them to Six Nations victory with a Grand Slam in 2009, their first since 1948.

Greatest player: Mike Gibson – a centre unlike any other, Gibson revolutionised the midfield game. He won 69 caps for Ireland during the 1960s and 1970s and scored a then world record of 112 Test points. His pace and vision were exceptional.

Biggest win: Ireland 83–United States 3 (2000).

Biggest defeat: Ireland 15–New Zealand 63 (1997).

Fan fact: Ireland sing two anthems before each home international match, *Ireland's Call*, which was composed in 1995, and *Amhrán na bhFiann*. For away matches, only *Ireland's Call* is sung.

Pocket fact H

Thomas Gisborne Gordon is the only player to have played international rugby with one hand. He represented Ireland in three matches during 1877 and 1878.

SCOTLAND

Founded: 1871.

Ground: Murrayfield Stadium, Edinburgh.

Honours: 14 Home Nations Championships (three Grand Slams).

Greatest coach: Jim Telfer – like his occasional coaching partner Ian McGeechan, Telfer coached Scotland for two periods between 1980 and 1999, leading to two Grand Slams and also winning the final Five Nations Championship in 1999.

Greatest player: Gavin Hastings – a rampaging, elusive full back with a monster boot, Hastings was also Scotland captain during his 61 appearances for his country. He set an overall points record of 733 points for Scotland and the Lions.

Biggest win: Scotland 100–Japan 8 (2004).

Biggest defeat: Scotland 10–South Africa 68 (1997).

Fan fact: Scotland have only ever won once in the southern hemisphere, beating Australia 12–7 in Brisbane in 1982.

WALES

Founded: 1881.

Ground: Millennium Stadium, Cardiff.

Honours: 24 Home Nations Championships (10 Grand Slams).

Greatest coach: John Dawes – with a 75% win success rate during his five years in charge of the national side, Dawes oversaw a golden era for Wales. The side won four championships during his reign, including two Grand Slams.

Greatest player: Gareth Edwards – Edwards won all his 53 caps consecutively, including 13 as captain, scoring 20 tries.

Biggest win: Wales 98–Japan 0 (2004).

Biggest defeat: Wales 13–South Africa 96 (1998).

Fan fact: 71 players with the surname Jones have represented Wales since the first international match in 1881.

FRANCE

Founded: 1906.

Ground: Stade de France, Paris.

Honours: 17 Home Nations Championships (nine Grand Slams).

Greatest coach: Jacques Fouroux – as well as winning a Grand Slam as a player in 1977, Fouroux led France to two Grand Slams and 6 Five Nations championships during his time as coach, plus the World Cup final in 1987 against New Zealand.

Greatest player: Philippe Sella – with 111 caps for his country and 30 tries to his name, Sella was one of France's greatest backs. His searing pace and vision on the field set him apart from other players.

Biggest win: France 87–Namibia 10 (2007).

Biggest defeat: France 10–New Zealand 61 (2007).

Fan fact: France had a 15-year break from international rugby from 1932 to 1947. They were excluded due to allegations suggesting payments had been made to players, creating professionalism when the game was still strictly amateur.

ITALY

Founded: 1929.

Ground: Stadio Artemio Franchi, Florence.

Honours: One European Nations Cup.

Greatest coach: Nick Mallett – whilst Italy remain a work in progress, Mallett has arguably brought out their best performances, including their greatest victory to date, beating France 22–21 in the 2011 Six Nations championship.

Greatest player: Diego Dominguez – Italy's main points scorer for over a decade, Dominguez racked up 983 points in 74 appearances for the Azzurri. The Argentine-born number 10 represented Italy at the 1991, 1995 and 1999 World Cups.

Biggest win: Italy 104–Czech Republic 8 (1994).

Biggest defeat: Italy 0–South Africa 101 (1999).

Fan fact: Former scrum-half Alessandro Troncon, who retired from playing in 2007, holds the record for international appearances for Italy with 101.

AUSTRALIA

Founded: 1899.

Ground: ANZ Stadium, Sydney.

Honours: Two World Cups, two Tri-Nations titles.

Greatest coach: Rod Macqueen – Australia's coach from 1997 to 2001, Macqueen finished with a win record of 80%, and led Australia to glory in the 1999 World Cup, the Tri-Nations for the first time, and also against the British & Irish Lions in 2001.

Greatest player: John Eales – Australia's most successful captain, playing in both World Cup finals, winning the Tri-Nations and beating the Lions.

Biggest win: Australia 142–Namibia 0 (2003).

Biggest defeat: Australia 8–South Africa 53 (2008).

Fan fact: Second World War hero Sir Edward 'Weary' Dunlop, who was imprisoned by the Japanese and renowned for his leadership, was part of the first ever Australian Bledisloe Cup winning side, playing second row in 1934.

NEW ZEALAND

Founded: 1903.

Ground: Eden Park, Auckland.

Honours: Two World Cups, 10 Tri-Nations titles.

Greatest coach: Sir Fred Allen – the oldest living All Black, he was head coach of New Zealand between 1966–1968 when they won all of their 14 matches, leaving him with an unbeaten record.

Greatest player: Colin Meads – the New Zealand Rugby Football Union's player of the century, Meads played without any break for New Zealand from 1957–1971 and was known around the world for his ferocious playing style.

Biggest win: New Zealand 145–Japan 17 (1995).

Biggest defeat: New Zealand 7–Australia 28 (1999).

Fan fact: Since 1903, New Zealand have won a remarkable 75% of their matches.

The Haka

Made famous by the All Blacks, Ka Mate *is a haka with Maori origins that is performed by each member of the New Zealand 22-man squad before the kick-off of any international match.*

*The haka is a traditional war dance or cry, which was per-
formed to intimidate enemies, normally before battle. There are
many kinds, not just that performed by the New Zealand team.*

*A story of overcoming death, the haka performed by the All
Blacks has become famous around the world and is an essential
part of the experience of seeing the All Blacks play. Other
countries including Samoa, Tonga and Fiji also perform their
own individual hakas before games.*

SOUTH AFRICA

Founded: 1891.

Ground: Ellis Park Stadium, Johannesburg.

Honours: Two World Cups, three Tri-Nations titles.

Greatest coach: Kitch Christie – the 1995 World Cup winning
coach finished his tenure with the Springboks with a 100% record
that included 14 consecutive victories.

Greatest player: Joost Van Der Westhuizen – the brilliant
Springbok scrum-half went to three World Cups, including the
successful 1995 campaign on South African soil, and finished his
career on 89 tests, having scored 38 tries – at the time a South
African record.

Biggest win: South Africa 134–Uruguay 5 (2005).

Biggest defeat: South Africa 3–England 53 (2002).

Fan fact: South Africa play with two emblems on their shirts, the
image of a springbok and, since 1992, the King Protea, an indigenous flower.

ARGENTINA

Founded: 1910.

Ground: Estadio José Amalfitani, Buenos Aires.

Honours: None.

Greatest coach: Marcelo Loffreda – Argentina's coach between 2000 and 2007, Loffreda led Argentina to a third-place finish in the 2007 World Cup, and an IRB ranking of third in the world, their highest ever placing.

Greatest player: Agustin Pichot – a popular player at club level for Stade Français, Richmond, Bristol and Racing Métro, Pichot was Argentina's talismanic scrum-half and captain, helping them shock the world in the 2007 World Cup.

Biggest win: Argentina 152–Paraguay 0 (2002).

Biggest defeat: Argentina 8–New Zealand 93 (1997).

Fan fact: From 2012 Los Pumas compete annually with South Africa, Australia and New Zealand in an expanded Four Nations tournament, the first time Argentina have been included in major international competition outside of the World Cup.

☉ THE BEST OF THE REST ☉

While the top teams are often regularly fighting it out for the game's top prizes, many other rugby-playing nations across the globe are on the rise and set to challenge the established sides by the end of the next decade. Here are the up and coming teams.

SAMOA

Founded: 1924.

Ground: Apia Park, Samoa.

Honours: One Pacific Nations Cup, nine Pacific Tri-Nations titles.

Greatest coach: Fuimaono Titimaea Taufua – the former Manu Samoa player led Samoa to Pacific Nations Cup glory in 2010 and to a famous victory over Australia in 2011, the first time Samoa had beaten an IRB top five ranked nation.

Greatest player: Brian Lima – fondly nicknamed around the world as 'the chiropractor', for his huge defence, Lima is

Samoa's record appearance holder with 62 and the record try scorer with 28. He also played in five World Cups from 1991–2007.

Biggest win: Samoa 115–Papua New Guinea 7 (2009).

Biggest defeat: Samoa 14–New Zealand 101 (2008).

Fan fact: Several Samoan-born players have chosen to represent New Zealand instead of Samoa, including Mils Muliaina, Isaia Toeava and Jerry Collins.

USA

Founded: 1912.

Ground: Infinity Park, Colorado.

Honours: Two Churchill Bowls, two Olympic Gold Medals.

Greatest coach: Tom Billups – the Eagles head coach at the 2003 Rugby World Cup.

Greatest player: Luke Gross – the USA's most capped player with 62, Gross stood out at 6ft 10in. He played for the Eagles between 1996 and 2003.

Biggest win: USA 91–Barbados 0 (2006).

Biggest defeat: USA 8–England 106 (1998).

Fan fact: The USA are the only side to have won Olympic Gold for rugby, succeeding in both tournaments when rugby was played at the 1920 and 1924 Olympics.

CANADA

Founded: 1932.

Ground: BMO Field, Toronto.

Honours: One Churchill Cup Plate, three Churchill Cup Bowls.

Greatest coach: Ian Birtwell – the English coach led the Maple

Leafs to the quarter-finals of the 1991 World Cup, against all the odds.

Greatest player: Gareth Rees – Canada's top points scorer with 487, Rees spent his club career with London Wasps and Harlequins in the Premiership.

Biggest win: Canada 71–Barbados 3 (2006).

Biggest defeat: Canada 0–England 70 (2004).

Fan fact: Canada have beaten close rivals the USA 32 times in 45 matches, securing their status as the best side in North America.

JAPAN

Founded: 1932.

Ground: Chichibunomiya Stadium, Tokyo.

Honours: One Pacific Nations Cup, four Asian Five Nations titles.

Greatest coach: Hiroaki Shukuzawa – led Japan to their most famous victory over Scotland 28–24 in 1989, as well as their only World Cup win, over Zimbabwe in 1991 by 52 points to 8.

Greatest player: Daisuke Ohata – test rugby's leading try scorer with 69, Ohata played for Japan from 1996 to 2011, when his career was cut short by injury.

Biggest win: Japan 155–Chinese Taipei 3 (2002).

Biggest defeat: Japan 17–New Zealand 145 (1995).

Fan fact: Former Japanese full-back Toru Kurihara holds the record for the most points in a match, scoring 90 (6 tries and 15 conversions) in a 120–3 win over Taiwan in 2002.

Pocket fact H

The highest recorded points score in an international match was in Kuala Lumpur in 1994 when Hong Kong beat Singapore by 164 points to 13.

TONGA

Founded: 1924.

Ground: National Stadium, Nuku'alofa.

Honours: Two Pacific Tri-Nations titles.

Greatest coach: Polutele Tu'ihalamaka – was in charge when Tonga beat Italy at the 1999 World Cup, and alongside Dave Waterston he led Tonga to a famous 20–16 victory over a strong France side, also in 1999.

Greatest player: Pierre Hola – Tonga's top points scorer with 286, Hola played as both a winger and a fly-half for the national side during a career that lasted over a decade from 1998–2009.

Biggest win: Tonga 119–Korea 0 (2003).

Biggest defeat: Tonga 0–New Zealand 102 (2000).

Fan fact: Tonga have played close rivals Fiji 80 times, losing over half of those matches with a win percentage of 29.5%.

FIJI

Founded: 1924.

Ground: Suva Stadium, Fiji.

Honours: Nine Pacific Tri-Nations titles.

Greatest coach: Illivasi Tabua – well assisted by Australian coaches Shannon Fraser and Greg Mumm, Tabua guided Fiji to their best ever World Cup finish as they defeated Japan and

Canada, before edging a 38–34 thriller against Wales to qualify for the quarter-finals.

Greatest player: Nicky Little – Fiji's record appearance and points scorer has been playing for the national side since his debut in 1996. With 652 points to his name and 67 caps, the fly-half has been an integral part of Fiji's success in the last two decades.

Biggest win: Fiji 124–Niue 4 (1983).

Biggest defeat: Fiji 0–New Zealand 91 (2005).

Fan fact: Fiji were the first to go through an unbeaten tour of New Zealand in 1939, when they won seven matches and drew one.

GEORGIA

Founded: 1964.

Ground: Boris Paichadze National Stadium, Tbilisi.

Honours: Four European Nations Cups, five Antim Cups.

Greatest coach: Claude Saurel – the Frenchman led Georgia to a famous win over Russia in 2002 in front of 45,000 fans, qualifying them for the 2003 World Cup for the first time.

Greatest player: Malkhaz Urjukashvili – the Georgian winger has 65 caps for his country and has scored more than 300 points at international level, including 18 tries.

Biggest win: Georgia 98–Czech Republic 3 (2007).

Biggest defeat: Georgia 6–England 84 (2003).

Fan fact: Georgia hold an impressive record over close rivals Russia, having won 13 of their 15 matches.

RUSSIA

Founded: 1992.

Ground: Krasnoyarsk, Siberia.

Honours: None.

Greatest coach: Nikolay Nerush – the coach of club side VVA-Podmoskovye led Russia to their first Rugby World Cup after finishing second in the European Nations Cup.

Greatest player: Alexander Khrokin – Russia's most capped player, the prop made 67 appearances and scored seven tries in a nine-year international career.

Biggest win: Russia 104–Denmark 7 (2000).

Biggest defeat: Russia 3–Japan 75 (2010).

Fan fact: Vasily Artemyev became the first Russian player to sign for an English club in 2011, when the international winger joined Northampton Saints.

ROMANIA

Founded: 1919.

Ground: Arcul de Triumf Stadium, Bucharest.

Honours: Nine European Nations Cup, five Antim Cups.

Greatest coach: Bernard Charreyre – the French coach led Romania to their best World Cup victory, winning 37–3 against Namibia in 2003.

Greatest player: Gabriel Brezoianu – with 71 caps to his name, scoring 26 tries, Brezoianu played at centre for Romania during three World Cups (1999, 2003 and 2007).

Biggest win: Romania 100–Bulgaria 0 (1976).

Biggest Defeat: Romania 0–England 134 (2001).

Fan fact: Romania have beaten Spain 26 times out of 27 attempts, a win record of 96.3%.

☉ SPECIAL TEAMS ☉

The following teams are famous around the rugby world but do not compete in any league or tournament. Playing for the teams is by invitation and considered one of the game's greatest honours.

BRITISH & IRISH LIONS

Touring every four years to one of Australia, New Zealand and South Africa, the British & Irish Lions are made up of the best players from Britain and Ireland. Their tours include a three match series against the national side of the host country, with warm-up matches leading up to it.

Founded: 1888.

Honours: 14 victorious Lions tours of Australia, New Zealand and South Africa.

Greatest coach: Sir Ian McGeechan – 'Geech' was involved in a remarkable seven Lions tours, two as a player and five in a coaching capacity. He coached winning Lions teams in Australia in 1989 and South Africa in 1997.

Greatest player: Willie John McBride – the Lions record holder for the most appearances, McBride toured with the Lions a record five times (1962, 1966, 1968, 1971, 1974), making 17 test match appearances. He was also captain for the successful 1974 tour of South Africa.

Biggest win: British & Irish Lions 109–Manawatu 6 (2005).

Biggest defeat: British & Irish Lions 6–New Zealand 38 (1983).

Fan fact: Being selected for the Lions means getting to wear the iconic red jersey, which has been the official one since 1950 after various experiments to incorporate each of the home nation's colours.

Pocket fact H

In September 1938, a London news agency was awaiting a wire from South Africa to confirm the score of the final test between South Africa and the Lions. The Springboks had been 13–3 up at half-time, so when the wire arrived reading 'SA 16–21 Lions' they assumed it was a mistake. They reversed the score to the expected outcome and reported a defeat, rather than an incredible comeback by the Lions.

THE BARBARIANS

An invitational side, the Barbarians bring together the best talent in world rugby, playing matches all over the world against both international and club sides.

Founded: 1890.

Greatest coach: Carwyn James – the mastermind behind the Barbarians' most famous victory against New Zealand in 1973, James had led the Lions to victory in their tour of New Zealand. According to novelist and Welsh rugby enthusiast Alun Richards, who wrote a biography of Carwyn James, 'his vision of what might be made him the coach of coaches'.

Greatest player: Tony O'Reilly – the Irish winger remains the holder of the record for the most Barbarians appearances and the top try scorer to date, with 30 caps and 38 tries, collected between 1955 and 1963.

Biggest win: Barbarians 84–Belgium 10 (2008).

Biggest defeat: Barbarians 11–Australia 60 (2011).

Fan Fact: The greatest invitational side in rugby, for over 90 years the Barbarians would annually take part in the Edgar Mobbs memorial match, in memory of Northampton and England captain Edgar Mobbs who was killed in the First World War.

6

TOURNAMENTS AND COMPETITIONS

There has been an increase in major rugby competitions since the 1980s, with the first Rugby World Cup and the opening of the game to professionals. Teams once played each other for status and pride, now there is plenty of silverware to go around as well.

⊕ INTERNATIONAL COMPETITION ⊕

Until the introduction of the Rugby World Cup in 1987, international rugby was played on tours, whilst countries that were close enough to each other geographically would play in annual competition, for example the Home Nations championship in the British Isles. As more countries have begun to show an interest in the game and developed into competitive forces though, the landscape of international rugby has changed significantly, with more teams competing for bigger prizes.

RUGBY WORLD CUP

Founded: 1987.

Number of tournaments: Seven.

Number of teams: 20.

Most successful team: South Africa (1995, 2007), Australia (1991, 1999), New Zealand (1987, 2011).

Biggest win: Australia 142–Namibia 0 (2003).

When and where

Held every four years in different locations around the world, the World Cup has been held so far in New Zealand (twice), South

Africa, Australia, England (three times) and France, with matches also being played in Wales, Scotland and Ireland. The next World Cups are to be held in England in 2015 and Japan in 2019.

How to qualify

Now featuring 20 teams, every side that finishes third or higher in the pool stages of the previous World Cup tournament automatically qualifies for the next tournament four years later. This means 12 of the available places are already taken, with the remaining eight places decided by qualification. Europe and the Americas are each allocated two qualification spots, with one spot each going to Africa, Asia and Oceania. The last place is decided by a play-off, which features two semi-finals between the runners-up from Europe, Asia, Africa and the Americas with the winner of the final qualifying for the World Cup.

The trophy

The World Cup trophy is named after the game's creator, William Webb Ellis, and has been presented to the winning team of the World Cup since the tournament's inception in 1987. Made of silver gilt and crafted by the then Crown jewellers Garrard, of London, the cup was nicknamed 'Bill' by the Australian World Cup winning side of 1991.

Impressive records

- **8:** Record number of tries scored in a single tournament, shared by Jonah Lomu (New Zealand) and Bryan Habana (South Africa).

- **126:** Most points scored in a single World Cup tournament was by Grant Fox of New Zealand in 1987.

- **8:** Number of successful penalty goals kicked by Matt Burke (Australia), Gonzalo Quesada (Argentina), Gavin Hastings (Scotland) and Thierry Lacroix (France) in a single match.

- **22:** Highest number of appearances at World Cups, a record held by Jason Leonard (England, 1991–2003).

- **22:** most tries scored in a single match by Australia against Namibia in 2003.

Pocket fact H

New Zealand's Marc Ellis scored the most tries in a World Cup match, scoring six against Japan in 1995.

The fourth-choice fly-half

Originally not part of the All Blacks World Cup squad in 2011, Stephen Donald ended up kicking the winning points to bring New Zealand their second global title. After Daniel Carter, Colin Slade were ruled out of the tournament, and Aaron Cruden was injured in the final, Donald came off the bench and kicked the winning penalty to make the score 8–7, completing a remarkable journey from his fishing trip to World Cup glory.

SIX NATIONS

Founded: 1883.

Number of tournaments: 111.

Number of teams: Six.

Most successful team: England – 26 victories, 12 Grand Slams.

Biggest win: England 80–Italy 23 (2001).

When and where

The Six Nations is the major annual international tournament in the northern hemisphere. It is played across the six participating countries (England, France, Ireland, Italy, Scotland and Wales), with teams playing either two or three matches at home during each tournament, depending on the fixture list.

How to qualify

There is no qualification for the Six Nations, each nation plays every year. France and Italy were added to the tournament by invitation, France in 1947 and Italy in 2000.

The trophy

As well as a main trophy for the outright winner of the tournament, there are other smaller trophies that are competed for between different pairs of nations.

- **Championship Trophy:** a cup made of sterling silver that was first presented to the then champions, France, in 1993. It was created by London firm William Comyns and is said to be worth £55,000. The inside is plated with 22-carat gold.

- **Triple Crown Trophy:** awarded to whichever of the four home nations has defeated the other three, the Triple Crown trophy is a silver dish that was commissioned by RBS, the tournament's sponsor. Before then, it was known as the 'invisible trophy' as no actual silverware existed.

The Calcutta Cup is also awarded to the winner of the match between England and Scotland during the Six Nations (see p.9).

Impressive records

- **35:** Most points in a match scored by Jonny Wilkinson of England against Italy in 2001.

- **551:** Most points scored in Six Nations history by Ireland's Ronan O'Gara.

- **25:** Most tries scored in the tournament's history by Brian O'Driscoll.

- **56:** The highest number of appearances in Six Nations history, held jointly by Mike Gibson and Ronan O'Gara of Ireland.

THE RUGBY CHAMPIONSHIP (WAS TRI-NATIONS)

Founded: 1996.

Number of tournaments: 15.

Number of teams: Four.

Most successful team: New Zealand (10 titles).

Biggest win: Australia 49–South Africa 0 (2006).

When and where

In 2012 for the first time four teams will feature in this annual tournament instead of the previous three, with Argentina being added to the tournament against Australia, South Africa and New Zealand. In non-World Cup years, each side has played the other two teams three times per tournament, with the winner being decided on a points basis in the table after six matches.

How to qualify

There is no qualification process for the Tri-Nations. Argentina, who gave an impressive performance at the 2007 World Cup, have been included for 2012 so they can continue the strengthening of their side through competing against the world's best teams on a regular basis.

The trophy

Crafted in the shape of the traditional cup with two large handles, the silver Tri-Nations Trophy has been presented to the winner of the tournament since its inception in 1996.

Impressive records

- **16:** New Zealand full-back Christian Cullen holds the record for the most tries in Tri-Nations history.

- **48:** Record number of appearances in the Tri-Nations is held by Australia's George Gregan.

- **46–40:** Highest scoring game in the Tri-Nations came in 2000 when South Africa beat New Zealand at Ellis Park, Johannesburg.

- **429:** Dan Carter, of New Zealand, holds the record for the highest number of points in Tri-Nations history.

PACIFIC NATIONS CUP

Founded: 2006.

Number of tournaments: Six.

Number of teams: Four/five.

Most successful team: Junior All Blacks.

Biggest win: Australia 142–Namibia 0 (2003).

When and where

The tournament was launched in 2006 to provide increased game time for the leading Pacific nations of Fiji, Samoa, Tonga plus Japan and the Junior All Blacks from New Zealand. It is normally hosted by one nation, and is now held on an annual basis.

How to qualify

There is no qualification for the Pacific Nations Cup, with the four core sides, Japan, Tonga, Fiji and Samoa, competing each year. Occasionally other sides have been invited to play in the tournament, including Australia 'A', the New Zealand Maori, and most recently the Junior All Blacks.

The trophy

The Pacific Nations Cup is made from silver with two handles, with a wooden base and a silver plaque on which the names of previous winners are engraved.

Impressive records

- **98:** Fiji's Taniela Rawaqa is the tournament's leading points scorer.

- **8:** Former Junior All Blacks player Hosea Gear holds the tournament's try-scoring record.

Pocket fact H

Twenty-one players have won more than 100 caps for their countries, the first to do so being centre Philippe Sella of France in 1995.

ASIAN 5 NATIONS

Founded: 2008.

Number of tournaments: Four.

Number of teams: Five.

Most successful team: Japan (four titles).

Biggest win: Japan 114–Arabian Gulf 6 (2008).

When and where

The Asian 5 Nations, featuring 24 teams across six divisions, is one of the most exciting new tournaments in world rugby. Teams are relegated and promoted at the end of each season. The tournament features evolving rugby teams such as Japan, Kazakhstan and Hong Kong through to minnows such as Cambodia, Laos and Brunei.

How to qualify

The teams are all selected by the Asian Rugby Union, meaning there is no qualification process. To play in the Top 5, the highest level of competition, teams must be promoted from Division I.

The trophy

Arguably the most spectacular trophy in world rugby, the Asian 5 Nations trophy is engraved with traditional Asian motifs, with two dragons' heads forming the handles. It was made in India by the silversmiths Whorra Brothers and donated to the tournament by the Calcutta Cricket & Football Club and Bombay Gymkhana club.

Impressive records

- **142:** Record for the most points by a single player in the Asian 5 Nations is held by Japan's Shaun Webb.

- **15:** Alisi Tupuailei has scored a remarkable 15 tries in just seven Asian 5 Nations matches.

EUROPEAN NATIONS CUP

Founded: 2000.

Number of tournaments: 11.

Number of teams: 35.

Most successful team: Georgia (four titles).

Biggest win: Romania 96–Portugal 0 (1996).

When and where

The largest tournament in world rugby, the European Nations Cup is second only in Europe to the Six Nations championship. The tournament is played in seven divisions with five or six teams in each. The tournament runs over two years, and teams which finish in first place in their divisions are then promoted and those that finish at the bottom are relegated.

How to qualify

There is no direct qualification for the European Nations Cup, given that all the European rugby teams are accommodated in one of the Cup's many leagues, from champions Georgia down to Azerbaijan in the lowest division.

The trophy

The trophy is a rectangular shield.

Impressive records

- **27:** Record for the most points scored in a match is held by Romania's Virgil Popisteanu against Portugal in 1996.

- **59:** Romania's Constantin Dinu holds the record for the most appearances in the competition, between 1965 and 1983.

- **17:** Manrico Marchetto of Italy holds the try-scoring record for the competition, having scored a try every two games.

IRB NATIONS CUP

Founded: 2006.

Number of tournaments: Six.

Number of teams: Six.

Most successful team: Emerging Springboks (two titles).

Biggest win: Argentina 'A' 64–Romania 6 (2006).

When and where

Apart from when Portugal hosted the first tournament in 2006, Romania has been the host for the last five annual IRB Nations Cups. Teams that have taken part include Romania, Georgia, Namibia, Russia, Uruguay, Portugal, as well as two teams from South Africa, the Emerging Springboks and the South African Kings.

How to qualify

Sides compete in the tournament by invitation. The make-up has changed almost every year as sides have pulled out and replacements added.

The trophy

Made of silver, the trophy is shaped like a rugby ball on a stand.

Impressive records

- **119:** Italy A's Luciano Orquera holds the record for the most points scored in the competition.

- **6:** Siyanda Grey of Eastern Province Kings is the tournament's top try scorer, despite only featuring in one tournament in 2011.

WOMEN'S RUGBY WORLD CUP

Founded: 1991.

Number of tournaments: Six.

Number of teams: 12.

Most successful team: New Zealand (four titles).

Biggest win: New Zealand 134–Germany 6 (1998).

When and where

The Women's World Cup has been contested since 1991, but was only officially recognised by the IRB in 2006. Twelve teams competed in the last World Cup in 2010, and the next one will take place in France in 2014.

How to qualify

The winners, runners-up, and third placed team from the previous World Cup automatically qualify, as do the hosts. There are then four more qualifiers from Europe, two from the Americas, one from Africa, one from Asia and one from Oceania.

The trophy

A similar mould to the English Premiership trophy, the Women's Rugby World Cup trophy is made of silver with two large loop handles on either side. In the centre on the front of the trophy the IRB Women's Rugby World Cup logo is engraved.

Impressive records

- **73:** New Zealand's Annaleah Rush holds the record for most points scored in a tournament, gained in 1998.

- **14:** Canadian full-back Heather Moyse has scored seven tries in both the 2006 and 2010 Rugby World Cups.

Pocket fact H

As well as being a very successful rugby player for Canada, Heather Moyse is an Olympic Gold medallist, having finished first in the two-woman bobsleigh at the 2010 Vancouver Winter Olympics.

WOMEN'S SIX NATIONS

Founded: 1996.

Number of tournaments: 15.

Number of teams: Six.

Most successful team: England (12 titles, 11 Grand Slams).

Biggest win: England 89–Scotland 0 (2011).

When and where

The same format as the men's Six Nations tournament, all six sides play against each other once either home or away. The participants today are also the same, although Italy have only been part of the Six Nations since 2007 when they replaced Spain.

How to qualify

Teams are included by invitation and cannot qualify for the Six Nations.

The trophy

Designed by Trevor Brown and made in London, the Women's Six Nations trophy has two distinctive handles and is made of silver.

Impressive records

- **190:** Non Evans, of Wales, holds the record for the most points scored in Six Nations Championship history.
- **92.7:** England's win percentage in Six Nations history.
- **14:** Number of Triple Crowns England have won out of a possible 16.

◉ DOMESTIC LEAGUES ◉

Aside from international competition, rugby's heart lies in the domestic leagues around the world, where town and regional pride remain strong motivators. Here are the world's top domestic competitions.

THE ENGLISH PREMIERSHIP

Founded: 1987.

Country: England.

Number of teams: 12.

First winners: Leicester Tigers.

Most successful team: Leicester Tigers (nine titles).

Biggest Win: Richmond 106–Bedford 12 (1999).

History

Leagues were finally introduced to English rugby in the late 1980s after years of resistance by the RFU. With the introduction of the league, there was no longer any doubt about which was the best team in the country.

Organisation of fixtures was left to the clubs, who for the first season were:

- Bath
- Bristol
- Coventry
- Gloucester
- Harlequins
- Leicester
- Moseley
- Nottingham
- Orrell
- Sale
- Wasps
- Waterloo

Of those 12 teams, only half now still play in the Premiership. Teams only played each other once, and it wasn't until 1994 that a home and away structure was set up. The season is now played from September through to the final in May.

The league has been a huge success, with bigger crowds season after season and a strong TV partnership with Sky Sports and now ESPN resulting in the game being shown to a nationwide audience.

Since the 2002–2003 season, the winner of the Premiership has been decided by a play-off system. The first-placed team in the league table plays the fourth-placed side in one semi-final, with second playing third in the other. The winners of both games meet at Twickenham stadium for the final.

Qualification

Aside from the teams who were included when the league was first formed, teams earn promotion to the Premiership by finishing as champions of the league below, the Championship. At the end of the season, the team that finishes last in the Premiership is relegated to the Championship, making way for the team promoted.

The trophy

One of the largest trophies in the world, the Premiership trophy is made of silver and weighs about 12.5kg. It was made by Asprey of London.

Impressive records

- **1,870:** Charlie Hodgson, now of Saracens but formerly of Sale Sharks, is the Premiership's all-time record points scorer.

- **75:** Steve Hanley holds the record for the most Premiership tries scored. He played for Sale from 1998–2008.

- **238:** Hugh Vyvyan is the Premiership's record appearance holder. He played for both Newcastle and Saracens.

- **17:** Richmond's Dominic Chapman holds the record for the most tries scored in one Premiership season, in 1997–1998.

Pocket fact H

Julian White, who has played for Leicester, Saracens and Bristol, has the worst disciplinary record in Premiership history, with seven yellow and five red cards.

THE CELTIC LEAGUE

Founded: 2001.

Country: Ireland/Italy/Scotland/Wales.

Number of teams: 12.

First winners: Leinster (2002).

Most successful team: Munster (three titles).

Biggest win: Cardiff 58–Connacht 0 (2008).

History

Created in 2001, the Celtic League was primarily designed as a competition for the Celtic sides from Ireland, Scotland and Wales. The first teams in the tournament were the four Irish provinces of Leinster, Munster, Ulster and Connacht, with Scotland fielding the two club sides Edinburgh Reivers and Glasgow, along with the Welsh club sides Bridgend, Caerphilly, Cardiff, Ebbw Vale, Llanelli, Neath, Newport, Pontypridd and Swansea.

However, with the introduction of regional teams in Scotland and Wales, the number of teams has decreased. Edinburgh and Glasgow Warriors are still the Scottish representatives, whilst the Welsh teams are the four regions of Llanelli (the Scarlets), Neath & Swansea (the Ospreys), Newport (the Dragons) and Cardiff (the Blues). Two Italian sides were added in 2010, Benetton Treviso and Aironi Rugby, to take the total number of teams to 12. The league is played from September through to the final in May.

Qualification

There is no relegation or promotion to the Celtic League. The two most recent additions to the league, Benetton Treviso and Aironi Rugby were invited into the league.

The trophy

The trophy is made of silver, with a Celtic band around the top decorated with blue, black and green stones.

Impressive records

- **130:** Deiniol Jones of Cardiff Blues holds the record for the most appearances in the league.

- **1,226:** Dan Parks of Cardiff Blues and formerly of Glasgow Warriors holds the overall points record for the league.

- **44:** No one has scored more tries than Tommy Bowe in the Celtic League, with his tally coming for both Ulster and the Ospreys.

- **14:** The record number of tries in one season was scored by Edinburgh's Tim Visser in 2010–11.

Pocket fact H

The highest attendance for a Celtic League game was when Leinster played Munster at the Aviva Stadium in 2010, with 50,654 fans turning out for the occasion.

THE TOP 14

Founded: 1892.

Country: France.

Number of teams: 14.

First winners: Racing Club de France (1892).

Most successful team: Stade Toulousain (18 titles).

Biggest win: Clermont 73–Dax 3 (2010).

History

Boasting the impressive record of being the oldest domestic rugby league in history, the Top 14 has existed since 1892. Only three teams have won the championship more than 10 times: Toulouse (18), Stade Français (13) and AS Béziers (11).

The number of teams involved in the league has changed over time, from the Top 8 to the Top 16 to the current structure of 14. The season is also the longest in world rugby, beginning towards the end of August and finishing with the final at the Stade de France in early June.

Qualification

Each season two teams are promoted from the league below, the Pro D2, the champion and the winner of the play-offs. The two lowest teams in the Top 14 are relegated at the end of each season to make way for the two teams coming up.

The trophy

The Bouclier de Brennus is the prize for the winners of the Top 14. A brass shield on a wooden support, the trophy was made by Charles Brennus ahead of the first final in 1892. A total of 27 teams have had their name engraved on the trophy, with the most recent new name being Clermont Auvergne, who won the title for the first time in 2010.

Impressive records

- **20:** Number of tries scored by Napolini Nalaga during the 2008–2009 season, two more than the whole of the Mont-de-Marsan team.

- **336:** Number of points scored by Racing Métro 92 fly-half Jonathan Wisniewski during the 2010–2011 season.

- **79,654:** Highest attendance for a Top 14 match, in the 2007 final between Stade Français and Clermont Auvergne, held at the Stade de France.

Pocket fact H
The league's governing body, the LNR, introduced a salary cap on the French sides for the first time ahead of the 2011–2012 season of €8 million, nearly double that of the salary cap imposed in the English Premiership.

HEINEKEN CUP

Founded: 1995.

Country: England/France/Ireland/Italy/Scotland/Wales.

Number of teams: 24.

First winners: Stade Toulousain (1996).

Most successful team: Stade Toulousain (four titles).

Biggest win: Stade Toulousain 108–Ebbw Vale 16 (1999).

History

The Heineken Cup is the biggest prize available domestically on the continent and the pinnacle of European club rugby. Held in a similar high regard to the Champions League in football, the competition was first proposed by the then Five Nations committee in 1995 in order to create a new level of European competition beneath the Five Nations championship.

The tournament is broadcast all over the world and beer company Heineken have sponsored the tournament since it began. Its popularity was exemplified by the attendance for the 2009 final between Leinster and Munster at Croke Park, which saw a club record of 82,208.

Qualification

All teams must qualify for the tournament, except the champions from the previous year, with 24 spots up for grabs. The top six teams in the English Premiership and the Top 14 qualify for the tournament, but if one of those teams has won either the Heineken Cup or the European Challenge Cup, then a seventh team is added from the same country.

Three teams are then picked from Ireland and Wales, with two from Scotland and two from Italy, and as with the English Premiership and Top 14, if one of those sides was the winner of the previous tournament, then their spot goes to the next best team from their country.

The trophy

Made by Garrard of London, the Heineken Cup is mainly silver, with platinum and gold features and a map of Europe on the front.

Impressive records

- **10:** Highest number of tries scored in one season, held by Brive's Sébastian Carrat in 1996–1997, the year Brive were crowned champions.

- **99:** Record number of appearances in the Heineken Cup, held by Munster's prop John Hayes.

- **1,196:** No one has scored more points in the competition than Munster's Ronan O'Gara, with the fly-half racking up this total from 1997 to present.

- **32:** Vincent Clerc of Toulouse is the tournament's all-time leading try scorer.

Pocket fact H

Six teams from France have contested a record 14 Heineken Cup finals, but only Brive and Toulouse have won titles. Perpignan, Colomiers, Stade Français and Biarritz have all fallen at the final hurdle.

EUROPEAN CHALLENGE CUP

Founded: 1996.

Country: England/France/Ireland/Italy/Portugal/Romania/Spain/Scotland/Wales.

Number of teams: 20.

First winners: Bourgoin (1997).

Most successful team: Harlequins (3 titles).

Biggest win: El Salvador 3–Brive 116 (2011).

History

Designed to accommodate the remaining European teams who had not qualified for the Heineken Cup, the European Challenge Cup began a year after the Heineken Cup in 1996. Over the years it has undergone various transformations, being known as the European Shield, the Parker Pen Shield, the Parker Pen Challenge Cup, to its present incarnation as the Amlin Challenge Cup.

Clubs that have played in the cup do not just include the original Six Nations teams, but the competition has also featured representative sides from Romania, Spain and Portugal in a bid to offer more teams across the continent the chance to play and to improve against regional opposition.

Qualification

The remaining teams in the English and French top flight leagues that do not qualify for the Heineken Cup automatically qualify for the tournament, including four teams from the Italian Super 10 league, as well as one side from Ireland, Wales and either Spain or Portugal and Romania's Bucuresti Oaks.

The winners of the five pools progress to the quarter-finals, where they face three teams who have dropped down from the Heineken Cup, normally the three sides with the most points that finished outside of the top eight.

The trophy

Designed by Asprey of London, the trophy is made of silver and was commissioned in 2002. It has a small bowl above a long shaft.

Impressive records

- **520:** Fly-half Ludovic Mercier holds the record for the most points scored in the competition, playing for an impressive five clubs: Petrarca, Gloucester, Grenoble, Pau and Béziers.

- **19:** Most tries in the tournament's history have been scored by Jean-Victor Bertrand, with the Frenchman touching down for Grenoble, Agen, Montpellier and Narbonne.

Pocket fact H

Castres have reached two European Challenge Cup finals, losing on both occasions in 1997 and 2000.

SUPER RUGBY

Founded: 1996.

Country: Australia/New Zealand/South Africa.

Number of teams: 15.

First winners: Auckland Blues (1996).

Most successful team: Crusaders (seven titles).

Biggest win: Bulls 92–Reds 3 (2007).

History

With the dawn of the age of professionalism in rugby union around the world in the mid-1990s, along with the creation of the Tri-Nations for the international sides, the governing body SANZAR (see Glossary, p.178) created a then 12-team provincial tournament to be played between the three countries.

Originally there were five teams from New Zealand, four from South Africa and three from Australia in the opening tournament in 1996. The Western Force side from Perth, Australia, were added in 2005, and the Central Cheetahs from Bloemfontein, South Africa, were also included the following year. The competition's current format was completed with the addition of the Melbourne Rebels in 2011.

Qualification

The teams that have been added to the tournament have done so by applying rather than qualifying. There is no promotion or relegation to Super Rugby, meaning that there is less pressure for teams to perform in order to stay in the league, resulting in arguably a brand of more exciting, attacking rugby.

The trophy

Designed by Blue Sky Design, based in Sydney, Australia, the current Super Rugby trophy is made of solid stainless steel. It weighs an impressive 18kg.

Pocket fact H

Wallaby and Melbourne Rebels winger James O'Connor holds the record for being the youngest player in Super Rugby. He made his debut for the Western Force against the Queensland Reds aged 17 years and 289 days in 2008.

Impressive records

- **148:** Former Queensland Reds hooker Sean Hardman holds the record for the most appearances in Super Rugby, racking up his total between 2000 and 2010.

- **1,174:** No one has scored more points in Super Rugby than Dan Carter for the Crusaders.

- **59:** Doug Howlett, now of Munster, scored more tries than anyone else in Super Rugby for the Auckland Blues from 1997 to 2007.

- **15:** Record for the most tries scored in a season is held by two players, Australian Joe Roff (Brumbies, 1997) and Rico Gear (Crusaders, 2005).

CURRIE CUP

Founded: 1889.

Country: South Africa.

Number of teams: 14.

First winners: Western Province (1889).

Most successful team: Western Province (32 titles).

Biggest win: Northern Transvaal 147–SWD 8 (1996).

History

One of the oldest competitions in world rugby; bar the gaps in play during the First and Second World Wars, the Currie Cup has been played consistently since 1889.

The tournament continues to attract huge interest in South Africa, with regional pride at stake, as well as around the world.

Qualification

The modern-day format of the Currie Cup has it split into two divisions, with eight teams contesting the Premier Division and six teams beneath them in the First Division. The Premier Division sides compete for the Currie Cup, while the teams in the First Division challenge for promotion to the Premier Division for the next season.

The trophy

The Currie Cup itself was not introduced until 1892. It was first held by the Griqualand West side after their match with a British Isles touring side in 1891. The British team were led by Sir Donald Currie, who proposed to give the trophy to the best South African side that his team faced during their tour. It has been contested by South African teams ever since.

Impressive records

- **1,699:** Record number of points scored in the competition by former Springbok fly-half Naas Botha, amassed between 1977 and 1992 for Northern Transvaal (now known as the Blue Bulls).

- **142:** No one has made more appearances in the Currie Cup than Helgard Muller, who racked up his total between 1983–1998, and all for the Free State Cheetahs.

- **74:** Former Golden Lions and Cavaliers winger John Daniels has scored more tries in the Currie Cup than any other player.

Pocket fact H

Jannie de Beer may be remembered for knocking England out of the 1999 World Cup with his drop kicks, but he should also go down in history for scoring an amazing 46 points in one Currie Cup match for the Free State Cheetahs against Northern Free State in 1997.

7

THE LEGENDS XV

In every game special players have come along who have transformed the landscape of the game and gone on to become global superstars. These players have stood out from the rest, so why not try and put them all in one team?

⊖ 1. OS DU RANDT ⊖

DOB: 8/7/1972.
Nationality: South African.
Position: Prop.
Teams: Free State Cheetahs, Blue Bulls, South Africa.

CAREER

A prop forward remembered as much for his long playing career as his muscular form, Os du Randt played for South Africa over 13 years, competing in three rugby World Cups (1995, 1999 and 2007), winning two titles in 1995 and 2007.

His renaissance in world rugby was remarkable. After missing nearly three years of rugby between 2000 and 2003 due to serious injuries, du Randt returned to playing for the Free State Cheetahs. His impressive form resulted in his recall to the Springbok setup by coach Jake White, and from then until the 2007 World Cup final he became an indispensable member of South Africa's World Cup team.

For du Randt to have started the final against New Zealand in 1995, and then the 2007 final against England in Paris 12 years later, was an incredible achievement, and one that made du Randt a cult figure around the world. The cries of 'Os . . . Os . . .' at

South Africa matches became part of the occasion of seeing the Springboks play.

REMEMBERED FOR: HIS SIZE

During the 2007 World Cup, du Randt measured up at an impressive 6ft 3 inches and 20 stone, making him a truly immense physical specimen. It was this size that gave him so much power in the scrum, and helped him earn such a big reputation around the world.

SOMETHING YOU DIDN'T KNOW

Du Randt effectively retired around the age of 27 when, crippled by injuries, he could not see himself continuing to play top-level rugby. It took a phone call from former World Cup winning team-mate Rassie Erasmus in 2004 to persuade him to play for the Free State Cheetahs, and the rest is history.

THE SECOND XV CHOICE: SYD MILLAR

A tighthead prop by trade but equally effective as a loosehead, Millar holds a remarkable record of playing 39 matches for the British & Irish Lions, including nine test matches. The Irish prop went on to become President of the IRB in 2003.

☒ 2. SEAN FITZPATRICK ☒

DOB: 4/6/1963.
Nationality: New Zealand.
Position: Hooker.
Teams: Auckland Blues, New Zealand.

CAREER

With an impressive record of 92 caps over an 11-year period playing for New Zealand, Sean Fitzpatrick is one of the true Auckland, All Black and world rugby legends. He made his debut in 1986 and impressed enough to be included in New Zealand's squad for the inaugural World Cup tournament to be held on New Zealand soil.

Due to an injury to first-choice hooker and captain Andy Dalton, Fitzpatrick broke into the side and kept his place all the way through the remainder of the tournament, starting the victorious final against France which New Zealand won by 29–9. He became a mainstay of the All Blacks side, and was awarded the captaincy in 1992. As a captain he is regarded as a great success, despite losing the 1995 World Cup final against South Africa at the death.

A winning series against the British & Irish Lions in 1993, and a rampant Tri-Nations victory in the tournament's first year in 1996 though secured Fitzpatrick's status as one of the All Black's greatest leaders. He also had success with the Blues in the first year of Super Rugby, with Fitzpatrick leading the provincial side to the first Super Rugby title.

REMEMBERED FOR: SOUTH AFRICAN SUCCESS

The All Blacks had never won a tour on South African soil until 1996, when under Fitzpatrick they won their three-match series against the new world champions, the Springboks, with two wins out of three. It won Fitzpatrick respect not just back home, but also in South Africa.

SOMETHING YOU DIDN'T KNOW

A hugely effective leader during his playing days, Fitzpatrick now runs a motivational speaking business.

THE SECOND XV CHOICE: KEITH WOOD

Irishman Wood won the respect of players and fans around the world for his all-action style of play. One of the most inspirational captains ever, he holds the records for tries scored by a hooker at international level, with 15.

☻ 3. JASON LEONARD ☻

DOB: 14/8/1968.
Nationality: English.

Position: Prop.
Teams: Saracens, Harlequins, England, British & Irish Lions.

CAREER

Another veteran of the scrum, Leonard competed in a remarkable four rugby World Cups for England (1991, 1995, 1999 and 2003), losing in the final, semi-finals and quarter-finals before finally tasting success in 2003 in Australia.

At one point Leonard was the most capped rugby player of all time, with his career ending on a total of 119 caps (including five for the British & Irish Lions). He remains the most capped England player of all time, having turned out for the national side from 1990 to 2004. He once won 40 consecutive caps for the national side, a then world record. He also captained England in 1996 against Argentina, a match in which he scored his one and only try for the national side.

REMEMBERED FOR: HIS DRINKING

Leonard was adored by the rugby public not just for his play-making but for his impressive drinking ability, and the stories that came with it. An old-school prop, Leonard has been quoted as saying: 'When I first started playing for England it was practically obligatory, especially as a forward, to drink as much as you could the night before a game.' He went on to compile an all-time rugby drinking XV, which can be found in his autobiography.

SOMETHING YOU DIDN'T KNOW

As Leonard was a player long before rugby turned professional, when he wasn't playing for either Barking or Saracens, he plied his trade as a carpenter.

THE SECOND XV CHOICE: GRAHAM PRICE

Another Lions legend, Price's career became legend after he ran the length of the pitch to score a try for Wales against France in 1975. He holds the remarkable record of starting 12 consecutive tests for the Lions, in 1977, 1980 and 1983, and not winning a single one.

⊖ 4. JOHN EALES ⊖

DOB: 27/6/1970.
Nationality: Australian.
Position: Second Row.
Teams: Queensland Reds, Australia.

CAREER

A second row unlike any other, Eales went by the clever nickname of 'Nobody', because 'Nobody's Perfect'.

At the time of his retirement he was the most capped lock forward in Test history on 86. This included an incredible 173 points for Australia, with two tries, 34 penalties and 31 conversions leaving him eighth on the all-time scoring list for his country. This kicking ability for a forward was unheard of before Eales, and remains so today, making him a completely unique player.

He was also part of two World Cup winning sides in 1991 and 1999, as well as Australia's Tri-Nations success in 2000 and 2001 and defeating the British & Irish Lions on Australian soil in 2001. Given that he was captain of the side during all of this success between 1999 and 2001, no captain has won Australia more silverware than Eales.

REMEMBERED FOR: THAT PENALTY

With time up in the final Tri-Nations match against New Zealand in 2000, Australia were trailing by a point when they won a penalty about 40 metres out from the New Zealand posts. The team's kicker, Stirling Mortlock, had left the field, leaving only captain Eales to send the ball over for the match. He lived up to his nickname, perfectly curling the ball through in order to win Australia not just the match but the Tri-Nations and Bledisloe Cup to boot.

SOMETHING YOU DIDN'T KNOW

Eales has a Bachelor of Arts degree, with a double major in psychology from the University of Queensland.

THE SECOND XV CHOICE: FRIK DU PREEZ

The Blue Bulls and South African second row was one of the great athletes on a rugby field, as well as possessing a mercurial boot that was the envy of many backs.

◉ 5. MARTIN JOHNSON ◉

DOB: 9/3/1970.
Nationality: English.
Position: Second Row.
Teams: Leicester Tigers, England, British & Irish Lions.

CAREER

When it comes to presence on the field, they don't come more imposing than Martin Johnson. The chief leader in a whole team of instrumental figures, Johnson's England team achieved unprecedented levels of success, with first wins in New Zealand and Australia and of course the World Cup success in 2003.

Johnson also enjoyed plenty of success at Leicester, leading the club to back-to-back Heineken Cup success in 2000 and 2001, as well as six Premiership titles. He is the only man to have captained two British & Irish Lions tours, in 1997 to South Africa and in 2001 to Australia.

All of these achievements make Johnson incredibly successful, even by the standards of this Legends XV. His immense strength and aggressive style on the field won the respect of everyone, from team-mates to fans, opponents to coaches. He is regarded as England's greatest player, and one of the best lock forwards of all time. In November 2011, Johnson stepped down as England Team Manager.

REMEMBERED FOR: HIS INSPIRATION

Arguably Johnson's finest moment of inspiration came against New Zealand in 2003 when, down to 13 men and defending a scrum on his side's own 5m line, Johnson implored his fellow forwards to 'get down and shove'. England hung on, sealing a first victory ever on New Zealand soil.

SOMETHING YOU DIDN'T KNOW

Although he was born in England, Johnson lived in New Zealand in his early twenties. Before returning to England and playing for Leicester, he played for King Country in New Zealand, and toured with the New Zealand U21s in Australia.

THE SECOND XV CHOICE: COLIN MEADS

One of the game's greatest enforcers, Meads had a presence that other locks envied, and between 1955 and 1971 won 55 caps for his country. Popularly known as 'Pinetree', he was voted New Zealand's Player of the Century in 1999.

Pocket fact H

New Zealander Jud Arthur was always a fan of the post-match sing-song. His team-mates gave him such an encouraging response to his renditions of Old Man River *and other ballads that he decided to pursue a singing career after an injury from rugby. He is now a professional opera singer based in Sydney.*

☺ 6. FRANCOIS PIENAAR ☺

DOB: 2/1/1967.
Nationality: South African.
Position: Flanker.
Teams: Transvaal, Saracens, South Africa, The Barbarians.

CAREER

Another of the game's great leaders, Francois Pienaar will always be remembered for his success with South Africa.

His career began with Transvaal in 1989, aged 22, before he made his debut for the Springboks in 1993. Pienaar was chosen to captain the side in his first Test match, and would go on to prove himself a superb leader. He won a Super 10 and Currie Cup double with Transvaal in the same year, but it would be two more years before Pienaar became a true legend of the game.

Now immortalised in the film *Invictus* (2009), Pienaar was inspirational in leading the 1995 South African team to World Cup glory, although he is just as famous for his relationship with Nelson Mandela. After this high he went on to play a key role establishing professionalism in South African rugby, before departing for England where he led Saracens to cup glory in 1998. He retired in 2000.

REMEMBERED FOR: UNITING A NATION

Pienaar, through taking South Africa to victory in 1995, helped lead the country into a new era of democracy and unity. Despite picking up a calf strain, he played on until the final whistle in the final, in which Joel Stransky's drop goal gave the Springboks a 15–12 victory after extra time. The sight of Nelson Mandela wearing Pienaar's number 6 shirt as he handed Pienaar the William Webb Ellis Cup became one of the sport's iconic images. Pienaar noted in his acceptance speech that the win hadn't been just for the 60,000 fans in Ellis Park, but all 43 million South Africans.

SOMETHING YOU DIDN'T KNOW

Pienaar's personal relationship with Nelson Mandela extends off the rugby field, as Mandela is godfather to one of Pienaar's two sons.

THE SECOND XV CHOICE: WAVELL WAKEFIELD

An English blindside flanker from before the First World War, Wakefield won 31 caps, including 13 as captain, and is regarded as the creator of the modern day flanking position with the way he hassled the opposition half-backs.

☻ 7. MICHAEL JONES ☻

DOB: 8/4/1965.
Nationality: New Zealand.
Position: Flanker.
Teams: Auckland Blues, Samoa, New Zealand.

CAREER

Another Auckland stalwart, Michael Jones made his debut for the side in 1985, aged just 20, scoring a hat-trick against South Canterbury. Although born and raised in New Zealand, Jones's first international cap actually came for his mother's home country, Samoa. He played for them just once, in 1986, before being selected to play for New Zealand ahead of the 1987 Rugby World Cup. The young flanker made his debut for the All Blacks in the tournament's first match, tasting victory in the 1987 final after playing in every round.

Serious injuries to his knees, along with refusing to play on Sundays on the grounds of his Christian beliefs, meant that Jones didn't play as many games as he might have done for New Zealand. He was hugely successful with Auckland during the 1990s, winning National Provincial Championships and five Super 6 titles. Renowned for his speed and big hits, he remains admired in New Zealand today.

REMEMBERED FOR: THE FIRST TRY

Jones will always be remembered for being the first player to score a try at the World Cup in 1987. There is a statue outside the Eden Park Ground in Auckland to commemorate the moment. He would also go on to score the first try in the next World Cup in 1991.

SOMETHING YOU DIDN'T KNOW

A devout Christian, Jones was not selected for the 1995 World Cup in South Africa on the basis that his stance of not playing on a Sunday meant he would have been unable to participate in the quarter and semi-final matches.

THE SECOND XV CHOICE: RICHIE McCAW

Another All Black openside, McCaw led New Zealand to glory in 2011 when they won the Rugby World Cup at Eden Park in Auckland, defeating France in the final. He is also the first All Black to reach 100 caps, and has won a remarkable amount of honours as captain of both New Zealand and the Crusaders, winning the Super 14, Bledisloe Cup, Tri-Nations.

◉ 8. ZINZAN BROOKE ◉

DOB: 14/2/1965.
Nationality: New Zealand.
Position: Number 8.
Teams: Auckland Blues, Harlequins, New Zealand.

CAREER

One of the most famous names in world rugby, Zinzan Brooke is remembered as one of the game's greatest ever number 8s. He made his debut as an openside flanker in the 1987 World Cup and was part of the winning squad in the final. He would go on to win 58 more caps for New Zealand between 1987 and 1997.

Blessed with serious speed and great kicking ability, Brooke was not your average number 8. He was one of the most complete players ever seen, with his all-round game marking him out as an exceptional talent. He finished his career on 17 test tries, a world record for a forward in international rugby.

As captain of Auckland he tasted great domestic success as well, winning the first two Super 12 championships in 1996 and 1997 with the Auckland Blues, as well as numerous NPC titles during the club's reign of supremacy in the 1990s.

Following the 1995 World Cup final, in which he played in the losing side, he moved to Harlequins in the UK before retiring after a stint with National League One side Coventry during 2002–2003.

REMEMBERED FOR: THE DROP-KICK

Brooke will be remembered for scoring a remarkable 47-metre drop goal in the World Cup in 1995 against England. Catching a high ball and on the run, Brooke simply hoofed the ball towards the posts, completing a feat that a back would have been proud of, let alone a number 8.

SOMETHING YOU DIDN'T KNOW

Brooke currently lives in Windsor, Berkshire in England, where he and his wife run a bed and breakfast business.

THE SECOND XV CHOICE: MORNE DU PLESSIS

Another player whose athletic abilities defied the number on his back, Morne du Plessis only won 22 caps due to South Africa's exile from international competition because of apartheid. He was captain for 15 of those caps, winning 13 of the matches, and was South Africa's team manager during the victorious 1995 World Cup.

⬭ 9. GARETH EDWARDS ⬭

DOB: 12/7/1947
Nationality: Welsh
Position: Scrum-half
Teams: Cardiff RFC, Wales, British & Irish Lions, The Barbarians

CAREER

Gareth Edwards's place in this Legends XV is no doubt well supported; he was voted as the greatest player of all time by *Rugby World* magazine in 2003.

His greatness is claimed by many to come from his excellent all-round athleticism, and the way he was able to convert a wide-ranging talent and utilise it best in rugby. Edwards was fast, possessed the finest of hands and was extremely accurate with the boot. On top of this, he was gifted with outstanding vision of the game, able to foresee opportunities where others couldn't.

Debuting for Wales aged 19 in 1967, Edwards earned 53 caps for his country, scoring 20 tries. His international career is all the more impressive given that he won all of his caps in succession, without any break in selection through loss of form or injury. He also won 18 caps for the British & Irish Lions, touring three times in 1968, 1971 and 1974, the latter being the unbeaten tour of South Africa when the Lions played 22 matches without loss.

However, Edwards is perhaps best remembered for his exploits for the Barbarians, making the famous black and white strip his own thanks to a memorable moment against the All Blacks at Cardiff Arms Park in 1973.

REMEMBERED FOR: THAT TRY

Edwards will always be remembered for one score in that 1973 clash. A team move that flowed from end to end, from Welsh fly-half Phil Bennett catching the ball on his own try line, through to Edwards diving in to score in the left-hand corner. It was as perfect a try as has ever been scored, and is referred to by fans, especially in the northern hemisphere, simply as 'that try'.

SOMETHING YOU DIDN'T KNOW

A keen fisherman, in 1990 Edwards held the British angling record when he caught a 45lb 6oz pike at Llandegfedd Reservoir in Wales.

THE SECOND XV CHOICE: GEORGE GREGAN

The most capped player of all time, Gregan won 139 caps for Australia between 1994 and 2007, playing in four rugby World Cups. His legendary partnership with Stephen Larkham at half-back became iconic, especially during the World Cup in 1999.

⊖ 10. JONNY WILKINSON ⊖

DOB: 25/5/1979.
Nationality: English.
Position: Fly-half/centre.
Teams: Newcastle Falcons, Toulon, England, British & Irish Lions.

CAREER

One of the game's most famous rugby faces, Wilkinson began his career in 1997 with Newcastle Falcons, joining the club after leaving his school, Lord Wandsworth College in Hampshire. The 18-year-old Wilkinson would go on to have an excellent debut season, resulting in his inclusion in the England squad and earning his first cap off the bench against Ireland in 1998.

The rest, as they say, is history, as Wilkinson has gone on to become not just one of the greatest fly-halves the world has ever seen, but also arguably England's greatest player of all time. Famed for his accurate goal and tactical kicking, as well his huge work in defence, Wilkinson's bravery in the tackle and compo-sure in attack won respect from fellow players and coaches. This icy level of control would see him go on to become the highest points scorer of all time in Test rugby, as well as winning the BBC Sports Personality of the Year award and IRB International Player of the Year award in 2003.

Wilkinson's career was blighted for nearly four years between 2003 and 2007, when he was sidelined by injuries to his shoul-ders, arms, knees and kidneys, meaning that he didn't represent England for three and a half years, with many fearing he would never return to his previous stellar form.

The career of the Surrey-born fly-half enjoyed an impressive ren-aissance in recent times. Since joining French side Toulon in 2009, a combination of climate and a fresh start rejuvenated Wilkinson, seeing him recapture some of his best form and become an integral member of England's squad, an accomplishment that has seen him represent his country at four rugby World Cups (1999–2011). In 2011, Wilkinson announced his retirement from international rugby having played 91 matches for England.

REMEMBERED FOR: THAT DROP-KICK

With seconds to go in the 2003 World Cup final, England and Australia were tied on 17-all coming up to the end of extra time. An English attack took the ball to inside the Australian 22, when Wilkinson, who had missed three previous drop goal attempts during the match, received the ball from half-back partner Matt Dawson and drop-kicked it through the posts to win England not just the match but the World Cup for the first time. It is a moment that has been re-enacted in many an English garden and rugby pitch ever since.

SOMETHING YOU DIDN'T KNOW

In his spare time Wilkinson is a keen guitarist, owning both a Gibson Les Paul and Fender Stratocaster, and has spoken of how he has often spent evenings before matches relaxing by playing the guitar.

THE SECOND XV CHOICE: HUGO PORTA

Porta single-handedly transformed Argentinean rugby. He was capped 58 times for Los Pumas and captained them in the first rugby World Cup in 1987. He retired aged 36 in 1990, completing 19 years of playing for the national team and scoring 651 points in the process.

Pocket fact H

Errol Tobias was the first black player to play for South Africa. He made his debut in 1981, when the apartheid regime still existed in the country. He played in six Tests for the Springboks, winning all of them.

☺ 11. JONAH LOMU ☺

DOB: 12/5/1975.
Nationality: New Zealand.
Position: Wing.
Teams: Auckland Blues, Waikato Chiefs, Wellington Hurricanes, Cardiff Blues, Marseille, New Zealand.

CAREER

An iconic winger of a type never been seen before, Jonah Lomu broke onto the world scene just as professionalism kicked in. His performances at the 1995 World Cup made him a global star, and he became respected by players and fans for his physical presence and turn of pace. His 120kg frame was complemented by raw speed. As a schoolboy Lomu had clocked an impressive time of 10.8 seconds in the 100 metres.

In all he earned 62 caps from 1994–2002, stealing the show at the 1999 World Cup with a series of impressive performances in the pool stages, notably against Ireland at Twickenham. There will probably never again be a rugby player like Jonah Lomu; his physicality and pace was a double-edged weapon as he either destroyed defences, or sucked them in to allow space for others.

However, his Superman abilities were constantly hindered throughout his career by kidney problems. In 1995, 1997 and finally in 2003, Lomu was sidelined by severe bouts of poor health, and by 2003 he was on dialysis three times a week.

REMEMBERED FOR: THAT 'TONGAN SIDESTEP'

Perhaps Lomu's most iconic moment came in 1995 against England at Ellis Park. Breaking down the left-hand touchline, Lomu was confronted by England full-back Mike Catt ahead of him, the last English defender before the tryline. Slightly off balance, Lomu simply bashed right through Catt, leaving him on the floor as he trampled over him and dived to score in the corner. It summed up Lomu perfectly: great footwork, pace and immense power.

SOMETHING YOU DIDN'T KNOW

Jonah Lomu's name also became synonymous with rugby video games, and 1999's *Jonah Lomu Rugby* on PlayStation is still hailed today as the best video game version of the sport.

THE SECOND XV CHOICE: RORY UNDERWOOD

No one has ever scored more tries for England than Rory Underwood, whose tally of 49 came in 85 appearances. Blessed with exceptional pace, he played in three World Cups and toured twice with the Lions, playing in six Tests.

⊖ 12. TIM HORAN ⊖

DOB: 18/5/1970.
Nationality: Australia.

Position: Centre.
Teams: Queensland Reds, Saracens FC, Australia.

CAREER

A double Rugby World Cup winner in 1991 and 1999, Horan played for Australia between 1987 and 2000, racking up 80 caps and scoring 40 tries.

A centre with excellent pace, Horan stood out in an impressive Australian backline during the 1990s, playing alongside first Jason Little and then Daniel Herbert for the Wallabies in the centres, and combining with half-backs George Gregan and Stephen Larkham to great effect in the victorious 1999 World Cup winning side.

In a sense, Horan set the standard for all future international centres in the professional game. He excelled in defence, was a brilliant play-maker – exemplified by the fact that he occasionally played at fly-half – and possessed exceptional pace.

His career was not without setbacks. He suffered a serious injury in 1994, severely damaging his knee, and there were doubts that he would go on playing. He went on to make the Australia squad for the 1995 World Cup, completing an impressive recovery.

REMEMBERED FOR: HIS CONTROL OF THE GAME

Australia's success in 1999 is often accredited to Horan and the way he controlled the play. His presence was never felt more greatly than during the semi-final against South Africa, when Horan continued to rip the South African defence apart. The fact that he had been struck down by food poisoning the night before means he is even more worthy of respect for his performance.

SOMETHING YOU DIDN'T KNOW

Horan won £10,000 during the 1999 World Cup from Guinness for scoring the fastest try, within 119.5 seconds.

THE SECOND XV CHOICE: DANIE GERBER

Another South African whose international career was blighted by apartheid, Gerber was hailed for his speed and raw power. He only collected 24 caps in 12 years, but impressed so much in this short space of time that he has never been forgotten.

13. BRIAN O'DRISCOLL

DOB: 21/1/1979.
Nationality: Ireland.
Position: Centre.
Teams: Leinster, Ireland, British & Irish Lions.

CAREER

One of Europe's greatest players and the finest centre of his generation, Brian O'Driscoll has become admired and respected around the world by fans and other players.

He has become a household name since his breakthrough international season in 2001, when he scored a hat-trick against France in Paris as a 21-year-old Irish centre fresh on the scene. As his career progressed, the pace faded slightly but O'Driscoll's talent and eye for a gap never left him. The more time went on, the more O'Driscoll started to find spaces where others wouldn't.

With this maturation as a player emerged an exceptional leader, as O'Driscoll went on to captain Leinster, Ireland, and most prestigiously the British & Irish Lions in 2005, before his tour was ended acrimoniously by Tana Umaga and Keven Mealamu (see p.31). He is the record try scorer for Ireland and holds the records for the most tries in the Six Nations and the Heineken Cup, as well as being the highest scoring centre of all time.

With over 100 caps, O'Driscoll's career has been unique. As he enters the twilight years of his career, it is certain that his status as a legend is already guaranteed.

REMEMBERED FOR: SCORING FOR THE LIONS

O'Driscoll has scored many a great try in his career, but one scored during the 2001 British & Irish Lions tour against Australia stands out. O'Driscoll was already a star in the northern hemisphere thanks to his exploits with Ireland, but he announced himself to the audience of world rugby with an amazing score against the Wallabies during the first Test at The Gabba in Brisbane. O'Driscoll spotted a gap between hooker Jeremy Paul and centre Nathan Grey and scorched through the two of them, before stepping replacement full-back Matt Burke with ease and racing under the posts. It was a try that underlined his immense talent, and a sign of things to come.

SOMETHING YOU DIDN'T KNOW

In 2011 O'Driscoll declined an invitation to the Royal Wedding because his club side Leinster were due to face Toulouse in the Heineken Cup semi-final the same weekend. His wife represented the couple on his behalf.

THE SECOND XV CHOICE: PHILIPPE SELLA

The owner of some of the finest footwork the game has ever seen, Sella was majestic. He won a then world record for international caps with 111 for France, scoring 30 tries in the process, over 15 years between 1982 and 1995.

⊛ 14. DAVID CAMPESE ⊛

DOB: 21/10/1962.
Nationality: Australia.
Position: Winger.
Teams: New South Wales, Australia.

CAREER

David Campese was one of the most talented players of his generation. Searing pace and incredible hands saw Campese do some extraordinary things on the rugby field.

In his 101 appearances for Australia over 14 years, Campese scored an impressive 64 tries, including nine during the 1991 Rugby World Cup, an achievement that led to his being voted Player of the Tournament. Although undoubtedly talented, he was also prone to making mistakes in big matches, including missing a series of kicks in a Test match against New Zealand in 1983. He also gifted the British & Irish Lions a try in the third Test of the 1989 tour of Australia, when he threw a wild pass that was gathered up by Ieuan Evans, leading to the Lions winning both the match and the series.

However, his genius outweighed the mistakes. He played a key role in the 1984 Grand Slam of the Home Nations, Australia's only one to date. The 1991 World Cup, though, was Campese's crowning glory, with his nine tries and famous assist for a Tim Horan try where he threw a pass over his shoulder cementing his reputation as one of the game's greatest wingers.

REMEMBERED FOR: THE CAMPO SIDESTEP

A variation on the classic sidestep became Campo's trademark, and was practised by thousands of rugby fans around the world. Running towards an opponent, he would momentarily slow down before with a kick of the leg accelerate off in another direction at full speed.

SOMETHING YOU DIDN'T KNOW

Campese berated the English arch-enemy many times during his career, and famously predicted that England had no chance in the 2003 Rugby World Cup final, and that he would walk up and down Oxford Street apologising and saying the best team won if they did. He kept his word.

THE SECOND XV CHOICE: DAISUKE OHATA

If a winger's job is to score tries, then statistically no one did it better than Ohata. Sixty-nine tries in 58 tests is a figure that defies belief, and although the Japanese player scored the majority of his tries against lesser opposition, his feat is impressive nonetheless.

⊕ 15. SERGE BLANCO ⊕

DOB: 31/8/1958.
Nationality: France.
Position: Full-back.
Teams: Biarritz, France.

CAREER

The only Frenchman in the XV, Blanco is one of the more tragic figures of world rugby. He was fiercely devoted to his club side, Biarritz, for whom he played from 1974 to 1992, but he never won a national championship, losing in his last game for the team in the final in 1992.

Internationally, however, Blanco was a great star of the game. In his 93 appearances for France he scored 38 tries, a national record that remains today. He also won three Grand Slams with France, as well as three more Championships, and was admired by all supporters for his running style and superb finishing skills. A very popular figure in France, Blanco became president of Biarritz after his retirement, with the club winning two National Championships during his reign in 2002 and 2006.

REMEMBERED FOR: THE EXTRA-TIME TRY

With France and Australia tied at 24 apiece going into extra time in the 1987 World Cup semi-final, both teams needed a moment of inspiration. For France, it came from the full-back Blanco. With France attacking in a wild manner with loose passes and high-risk running, space started to open up in the left-hand corner of the pitch. The ball was flung wide to Blanco, who sped for the corner and touched down incredibly close to the touch-line. The try was scored, and France went on to face New Zealand in the final.

SOMETHING YOU DIDN'T KNOW

Blanco grew up in France but was actually born in Caracas, Venezuela in 1958.

THE SECOND XV CHOICE: J P R WILLIAMS

Remembered almost as much for his sideburns as his skills, John Peter Rhys Williams lit up world rugby while playing for the all-conquering Wales side of the 1970s. He won three Grand Slams in 1971, 1976 and 1978, winning 55 caps for Wales and eight for the Lions.

Pocket fact H

No player has ever been left stuck on 99 international caps. However, former France hooker and captain Raphael Ibanez retired on 98.

8

STADIUMS

Rugby has come a long way since it was played on muddy fields in school grounds. Today, thousands of spectators regularly file in to world-class stadiums around the globe to watch their teams play. The biggest venues in the world of rugby play host to the national teams, where club rivalries are put aside and fans unite to cheer on their countries.

☺ TWICKENHAM ☺

Location: Twickenham, London, England.
Built: 1907.
Home team: England.

After playing their matches at Crystal Palace during the early 1900s, the RFU sought to build their own stadium. The first steps in Twickenham's creation were taken when William Williams purchased the 10¼-acre piece of land where the stadium now stands, at a cost of £5,572.

The first international match was held between England and Wales in 1910, and since then the stadium has hosted international games for over 100 years. This has included matches for the 1991 and 1999 rugby World Cups.

Twickenham also plays a major role in hosting domestic matches. The Premiership final is held at Twickenham ever year, as are national and county cup finals throughout the year. The stadium is also the setting for matches played by the Barbarians, and has hosted the Heineken Cup final on many occasions. Twickenham has also been the venue for some huge concerts, including The Police, R.E.M. and the Rolling Stones.

Pocket fact H

Twickenham can accommodate a crowd of 82,000, more than four times the capacity when the stadium first opened in 1910.

☺ MURRAYFIELD ☺

Location: Edinburgh, Scotland.
Built: 1925.
Home team: Scotland, Edinburgh Rugby.

Scottish rugby matches were moved to Murrayfield from Inverleith in 1925, with the first visitors being England in the Home Nations Championship. It has hosted rugby matches ever since, including two Heineken Cup finals in 2005 and 2009.

The current capacity is 67,130, making it one of the largest arenas in Scotland, meaning it is also frequently used for concerts as well as rugby matches. One of the legs of the Live 8 concert was held at Murrayfield, whilst Bon Jovi toured there in 2011, as have British rock group Oasis. Local football team Hearts have also used the stadium for European football matches, including a pre-season friendly against FC Barcelona in 2008.

Pocket fact H

Murrayfield is one of the few stadiums in world rugby to have an athletics track within it, with a 100-metre running track along the main stand.

☺ MILLENNIUM STADIUM ☺

Location: Cardiff, Wales.
Built: 1999.
Home team: Wales, Cardiff Blues.

Hailed by many as the greatest rugby stadium in the world, the Millennium Stadium was constructed in the late 1990s in time for the 1999 Rugby World Cup.

The stadium was built on the site of the old national stadium at a cost of £121m and is a testament to modern architectural standards with its retractable roof and three-tiered seating.

It opened for the first time in June 1999, only three-quarters finished, for a Test match between Wales and South Africa. By the time the World Cup began a few months later the stadium was complete, and the retractable roof was used for the first time during the opening ceremony of the 1999 Rugby World Cup. During that tournament the stadium was used for seven matches, including the final, which saw Australia beat France.

Pocket fact H

When Wembley Stadium was being re-developed between 2001 and 2006, the Millennium Stadium became the venue for the FA Cup Finals and Semi-Finals.

STADE DE FRANCE

Location: Saint-Denis, Paris, France.
Built: 1995.
Home team: France, Stade Français.

The fifth-largest stadium in Europe, the Stade de France has been used almost constantly by the French national rugby and football teams. It opened in 1998 in time for the football World Cup, which France hosted and won, beating Brazil 3–0 in the final. It was also the venue for the Rugby World Cup final in 2007 between England and South Africa, the semi-final between England and France and the opening match between France and Argentina.

Domestically, local side Stade Français have regularly used the stadium for big Heineken Cup matches, whilst domestic cup finals for both rugby and football are played there, as well as the final of the Top 14. The stadium is designed so that each of the 81,338 spectators is covered.

Pocket fact H

The Stade de France was constructed at a staggering cost of around €290m (approximately £254m), of which €45m (around £39m) was spent on the stadium's roof alone.

AVIVA STADIUM

Location: Lansdowne Road, Dublin, Ireland.
Built: 2010.
Home team: Ireland, Leinster.

Standing on the site of the old Lansdowne Road stadium, which was built in 1872 and demolished in 2007, the stadium is officially called the Aviva Stadium for sponsorship reasons until 2019, but supporters often still refer to it by the old name of Lansdowne Road. It is jointly owned by the IRFU and the Irish football authority, the FAI, with both national sides playing their matches there.

Built at a cost of €410m (about £359m), including €191m (approximately £167m) of government funding, the stadium has a capacity of only 51,700, making it significantly smaller than other elite stadiums in Europe. It is set to host the 2013 Heineken Cup final.

Pocket fact H

The stadium is unique in that its north stand features only one tier of seating. This is so that it does not loom over nearby housing and block out the light.

ELLIS PARK

Location: Johannesburg, South Africa
Built: 1928
Home team: South Africa, The Lions, Golden Lions

The famous venue for the final of the 1995 Rugby World Cup, Ellis Park is South Africa's major sporting stadium, situated in Johannesburg, its biggest city. Now known as Coca-Cola Park for sponsorship reasons, it was originally named after J D Ellis, who acquired the land on which the stadium now sits.

Today it is the host stadium for rugby matches featuring the national side of South Africa as well as Super Rugby side the Lions, and the Currie Cup team, the Golden Lions. The football team the Orlando Pirates also plays in the stadium. Ellis Park was used extensively during the FIFA 2010 World Cup, hosting one of the quarter-final matches between Paraguay and eventual champions Spain. It was first built at a cost of 40 million Rand (about £3.6m).

Pocket fact H

Approximately 3.1 million bricks were used in the building of the stadium in the 1920s.

☻ STADIUM AUSTRALIA ☻

Location: Sydney Olympic Park, New South Wales, Australia.
Built: 1999.
Home team: Australia, New South Wales Waratahs.

Formerly known as the Telstra Stadium and currently as the ANZ Stadium, Stadium Australia was specially built for the Olympics in 2000. Its general capacity is 83,500, although during the Olympics it was considerably more, with up to 110,000 people in the stadium at one time.

Today it is used for rugby league, Australian Rules Football and rugby union matches, as well as Twenty20 Cricket. The Australian soccer team also use the stadium for major international matches, and it was the venue for their play-off match against Uruguay in 2005 which resulted in them heading to the 2006 FIFA World Cup.

The stadium has hosted four national rugby league teams over the years: West Tigers, St George Illawara Dragons, and currently the Canterbury-Bankstown Bulldogs and the South Sydney Rabbitohs. Stadium Australia is the venue for the New South Wales State of Origin matches against Queensland since 1999.

The total cost of the stadium when first built was A$690m (about £450m), with a further A$80m spent on reconfiguring the stadium's capacity following the Olympic games.

Pocket fact H

At one point the stadium held the world record attendance for a rugby union match when 109,874 people watched New Zealand defeat the Wallabies in the 2000 Bledisloe Cup.

⬗ EDEN PARK ⬗

Location: Auckland, New Zealand.
Built: 1900.
Home team: New Zealand, Auckland Blues, Auckland.

In use since the turn of the 20th century, Eden Park has played host to cricket matches since 1910, and it is the only stadium to have ever hosted two Rugby World Cup finals, in 1987 and 2011. It is the current home of Super Rugby side the Auckland Blues, while ITM Cup side Auckland also play their home matches at the stadium.

With a capacity of 47,500 it is one of the smaller stadiums in world rugby, but the largest in New Zealand. Temporary seating enabled the capacity to increase up to 60,000 during the two Rugby World Cups.

Pocket fact H

The All Blacks have a win record of more than 80% at Eden Park, making it one of their more preferred venues. They have not lost a match there since 1994.

Top exotic locations to watch rugby

Watching rugby doesn't have to be all about sipping cups of tea and eating Cornish pasties on rainy nights in Newport, sampling the delights of the British weather in December. There are more exotic locations around the world where the location is as exciting as the game itself.

Suva, Fiji

A favourite stop for gap year travellers and holiday makers, the Pacific Island of Fiji is one of the great rugby locations in the world. The National Stadium in Suva is the home of the national team, whilst the Fijian capital has scorching temperatures above 30 degrees centigrade all year round.

Buenos Aires, Argentina

The Estadio José Amalfitani in Buenos Aires is the home of the Argentinian national team as well as local football side Vélez Sársfield. A former venue for concerts by Queen and Iron Maiden, it is situated just outside the bustling city centre.

San Sebastián, Spain

The occasional home of Basque side Biarritz, San Sebastián is situated on the northern coast of Spain near the French border. The Anoeta Stadium is just outside the city centre, with the town itself famous for its excellent tapas and Bay de la Concha.

9

PLAYING THE GAME

If you're feeling inspired to play the game, this chapter will outline everything you need to get started. What are those funny hats on some players' heads? What skills should you practise first? Read on and find out.

⬤ ESSENTIAL KIT ⬤

It is impossible to play a game of rugby without the following items.

SHIRT

Rugby shirts have undergone a radical transformation over the years, from the heavy cotton, single colour shirts with large collars, to the sponsor-laden, slim-fitting jerseys worn by teams around the world today.

Back in the 1870s, an everyday shirt would have been worn by the players with the addition of a bow tie and a coloured vest to distinguish one side from the other. As the game began to require greater athleticism during the turn of the 20th century, the bow ties and vests were discarded.

This style of shirt existed in one form or another until the 2000s, when the traditional collared shirt was replaced by modern skin-tight tops. Leading kit manufacturers such as Nike and Adidas claimed that the new shirts made players harder to tackle and also reduced the players' sweat levels on the pitch. This helped prevent over-heating and meant the players felt less restrained by the old baggy shirts.

In the amateur game today, shirts are still made of cotton and polyester and are buttoned at the top, although some teams pay more to kit manufacturers for similar skin-tight designs to those worn by professional teams. In bad weather, the weight of the traditional cotton shirts increases considerably, making them harder to train or play in.

The numbers

Shirts in the modern era have numbers on the back to identify a player's position. Previously, a lettering system was used, with 'A' meaning the loosehead prop, 'B' the hooker, and so on. Nowadays, the numbers run from 1, meaning the loosehead prop, to 15 for the full-back.

The numbering system was first introduced in 1950, but in reverse to the system used today, with number 1 representing the full-back through to the number 8 wearing 15. In 1960 the current numbering system was put into place.

Pocket fact H

Leicester Tigers and Bristol Rugby continued to use the lettering system until the late 1990s, labelling players A to O as opposed to numbering them 1 to 15. They they changed to use numbers like everyone else.

SHORTS

Rugby was first played in full-length trousers, but as they became increasingly troublesome to wear whilst playing, players sought alternatives by shortening the length to create rugby shorts.

The longer and baggier the shorts were the easier it proved to pull an opponent back, and so the length of rugby shorts has become shorter as the game has evolved. Today, shorts are made from high grade polyester with an elastic waist. Sponsors also regularly display their logos on the side or front of the shorts.

SOCKS

Long socks are used by modern rugby teams, though they may be rolled down depending on the player's preference. Again made from a combination of cotton and polyester, the socks are elasticated so that they stretch them over the calf muscles. They are either the same colour as the club's shirt or shorts, or a combination of the two.

SPONSORSHIP

Sponsorship has played a significant part in the transformation of rugby union shirts, with certain teams having several sponsors' names or logos on the front, back and sleeves of the shirt. Club sides sometimes feature the names of local businesses (who often subsidise the kit) or even local charities, helping to raise awareness. National sides normally feature big-name brands such as O2, ABSA, Qantas and RBS.

BOOTS

Rugby boots have changed dramatically over the years. The current cylindrical shaped studs have been used since 1910, and a modern rugby boot uses sets of either six or eight studs. The boots are traditionally made of leather.

Much like their footballing counterparts, players today are often sponsored by leading boot manufacturers including Nike, Adidas and Puma to wear their latest range of boots, resulting in some outlandish colours and styles now being found on rugby pitches around the world.

Pocket fact H

Leading All Blacks players Dan Carter and Richie McCaw have their own individual contracts with Adidas after signing million-dollar contracts with the company in 2004. As a result they are supplied with kit, from boots to training gear.

MOUTHGUARD

Although used in many contact sports, mouthguards have become essential in rugby due to the physicality of the sport. They are used to prevent any damage to the mouth area whilst playing, including the loss of teeth.

Available in a variety of bright colours many feature unique designs, from country's flags to fluorescent stripes. Made from ethylene-vinyl acetate, they can either be fitted professionally by a dentist or purchased at a sports store and moulded at home using boiling water. To fit the mouthguard at home it needs to be placed in hot water for a couple of minutes, before the player bites down leaving his teeth formation in the mouthguard, and then left to set.

Pocket fact H

The sponsors of the England rugby team, O2, have paid an estimated £36.5m for their logo on the shirt since 1995, when the company was known as BT Cellnet. The latest deal, signed in 2008, was for £4m a season, running until the end of August 2012.

☺ THE BALL ☺

The rugby ball's most distinctive feature is its shape. Often described as being egg-like, the oval shaped ball's dimensions originate from the days when pig's bladders were used to make the balls.

From this early model the shape of the ball has been refined with the passing of time, with the end becoming more curved in order to create two points at each end. Today rugby balls are made of very different materials from their original counterparts. An inner layer of cotton and polyester is glued together and is covered by a layer of rubber, designed to improve the gripping of the ball. Latex is used instead of a pig's bladder to make up the inner area of the ball and the four plates of the ball are stitched together.

Rugby balls have also decreased in general size; IRB regulations now require that a full-sized rugby ball must be 28cm–30cm (11–12in) long, and 58cm–62cm (23in–24in) all around at its widest point.

Pocket fact H

The official Rugby World Cup ball at the last five World Cups, from 1995 to 2011, has been made by Gilbert, and the same company is contracted to produce the official ball for the next World Cup in 2015.

⊙ EXTRAS ⊙

Aside from the basic items of kit listed above, in the modern game players use many other optional pieces of kit that may not be essential but are a good extra either for protection or to cope with previous injuries.

SCRUM CAP

Scrum caps have been used by players for decades, and are now becoming an iconic part of the game.

The caps are mainly used by forwards in the scrum, principally the tight five (props, hooker, and second rows) in order to prevent the condition known as 'cauliflower ears' (see p.19). By wearing the caps, the players prevent the rubbing of their ears that can lead to blood clots.

Players also use scrum caps in order to prevent severe head injuries during the match, as the padding inside the helmet cushions any blows to the head which may occur during tackles or rucks. For this reason, any player from 1 to 15 can wear a scrum hat, not just the forwards.

SHOULDER PADS

Shoulder pads help reduce the level of impact on the shoulder felt during tackles. By padding out the shoulder area one each side, the impact is reduced, lessening the risk of shoulder injuries such as trapped nerves or dislocations.

SKINS

An extension of the shoulder pads, players today often wear a long sleeved, skin-tight top underneath their playing shirt. These 'skins' help control body temperature whilst on the pitch and are preferable in the winter as an extra layer.

COMPRESSION SHORTS

The same as cycling shorts, these shorts are made of a spandex (Lycra) material and are worn underneath the playing shorts to prevent muscle strain in the thighs and to prevent chafing.

GLOVES

Gloves are worn to help a player's handling skills, improving the grip when passing or catching. They are favoured by hookers who throw the ball into the lineout and have the added advantage of keeping the hands warm in winter.

TAPE

Tape can be a simple substitute for a scrum cap, with players simply binding the tape around their head to protect their ears. This was more common in the decades before modern scrum caps were introduced, hence the iconic photos of forwards such as Willie John McBride and Bill Beaumont wearing big bands of tape on their head. Tape can also be used to hold up socks and secure shorts, or on the hands to prevent injuries to the fingers.

ELASTIC THERAPEUTIC TAPE (ETT)

The latest invention to be used within rugby, ETT, otherwise known as Kinesio Tape, is used to help heal previous injuries and offer immediate relief to damaged or strained muscles. Made in an electric blue or red colour, it is often worn by players on their thigh, calf or hamstring muscles.

◉ WHERE TO GET IT ◉

Now you know what you need, where can you get it? Here is a list of the top outlets for rugby kit.

- **Lovell rugby**: established nearly 25 years ago, Lovell rugby is an internet retailer for all things rugby, from balls to replica shirts to boots. Renowned for its wide range of international representative kits, from the All Blacks home kit to the Bali Sharks World Beach rugby shirt (www.lovell-rugby.co.uk).

- **Rugby Store**: based in the UK, the Rugby Store is one of the first to have all-new international and club kits exclusively in stock at competitive prices (www.rugbystore.co.uk).

- **Shoprugby.com**: with their flagship store in St Mary's Street, Cardiff, Shop Rugby is the first stop for all Celtic League and Six Nations international shirts (www.shoprugby.com).

- **Cotton Traders:** kit sponsors of many leading Premiership teams as well as the Barbarians, Cotton Traders are also producers of classic country kits from the past in the old-school style (www.cottontraders.co.uk).

- **World Rugby Shop:** linked with South African rugby, USA rugby and the All Blacks, World Rugby Shop is the leading world rugby retailer, operating out of Birmingham, Alabama and sending products all over the globe (www.worldrugbyshop.com).

◉ FINDING A CLUB ◉

As rugby continues to grow across the world, it has become easier for players to sign on with local clubs. The easiest way to find a local club is through the national governing body, who provide a list of clubs available in your area.

The governing bodies of the home nations have a feature on their website enabling players to search for clubs by simply entering their postcode in a search bar. The website then comes up with a list of local clubs, with such details as whether they have disabled access or women's rugby as well.

- England: www.rfu.com
- Ireland: www.irishrugby.ie
- Scotland: www.scottishrugby.org
- Wales: www.wru.co.uk

Pocket fact H

If you want to set up your own club and join a league remember that any new clubs must submit an application to the national governing body if they wish to join a league.

⊜ KEY SKILLS ⊜

Every rugby player has to practise in order to improve, and even more so if they want to be the best. No one typifies this work ethic more than professional players such as England fly-half Jonny Wilkinson, who is well-known for the long hours of practice he puts in to perfect his goal-kicking. While the average rugby player may not need to train this much, here are some key skills to practise.

PASSING

No one man can win a rugby match on his own, so being good at passing the ball is vital. A pass does not simply involve throwing the ball with your hands, but using the movement of your body and your hips to direct the pass. Face your target, and then swing the ball with two hands across your body. Spending half-an-hour practising passing with a friend is the easiest way to improve your technique.

CATCHING

One of the simplest actions in the game can sometimes prove to be one of the hardest. The trick is to practise by either throwing the ball in the air and catching it yourself, or by passing and catching with another person. Remember to keep your arms out in a basket shape to catch the ball, never taking your eye off the ball as it comes towards you. Practising how to catch under the high ball is best achieved by kicking the ball to one another, trying to re-enact a game situation as much as possible.

TACKLING

Better practised on tackle bags than on friends or siblings, tackles must be carried out below the waist for one simple reason: that's where they are most effective. It does not matter how tall the person is who you are trying to bring down, if you take out their legs, then they will fall. Practise using both left and right shoulders in order not to put yourself at a disadvantage on either your left or right side. When practising on a tackle bag, aim for no higher than halfway.

KICKING

This is more important for backs, though some forwards still love to pretend they're experts. Practising connecting with the ball is essential to ensure that mistakes are avoided during the match. This means practising kicking at the posts, for the corners, drop kicks, up and unders, as well any grubber kicks.

For the cleanest contact, you want to use the instep of the boot, following through with your whole body for the most power. For grubber kicks, however, you want to aim to hit the ball with the toe of your boot.

Warm up

It is very important to remember to warm up and warm down before and after any type of serious practice in order to prevent strains to important leg or upper body muscles.

RUGBY CULTURE

Rugby is as popular around the world for its physicality on the pitch as it is for its camaraderie off it, with tales of drinking, singing and eventful tours forming part of the fabric of the game's legend.

⬭ CLUB LIFE ⬭

A successful local rugby club is run not just on finances but on spirit. Everyone plays a part in making a club a venue to play rugby and a second home. From the players themselves, to the coaches, groundsmen and tea ladies, there are plenty of cogs in the machine.

COMMITTEE

Regular meetings are held between key people in the club in order to assess how the team is being run. Members of this committee will include a chairman, treasurer, secretary, coach and a players' representative so that all areas of the club are represented. It is the committee's role to organise events, tournaments and end of season tours.

AGM

The Annual General Meeting takes place in order to assess the previous year at the club, and includes the electing of officials as well as a report on the club's finances.

END OF SEASON DINNER

A big highlight on the social calendar. The end of season dinner is a celebration of a club's achievements throughout the season.

Dinners may also feature entertainment from comedians or other performers, and include a series of awards for players who have made an excellent contribution to the club. These include:

● Player of the Year

● Most Improved Player of the Year

● Coach of the Year

● Team of the Year

SOCIALS

Key to rugby club life are the weekly socials. Normally held after matches and occasionally with the opposition sides, socials involve a series of drinking games and songs and ensure that everyone has a good time.

⊛ THE RUGBY TOUR ⊛

At the heart of rugby camaraderie lies the rugby tour, a tradition carried out since the early 1900s by international and club teams travelling all over the world. Whilst each tour will no doubt be different, here are some essentials to make the perfect rugby tour.

TYPES OF TOUR

Depending on the level of rugby being played and the status of the team, there are different types of rugby tour:

Club tour

Given that most clubs operate on a relatively small budget, mainly on funding from the governing body and income from match-day revenue, the majority of rugby tours are not as extravagant as, say, the British & Irish Lions travelling to South Africa. Therefore, picking a destination is crucial to ensuring both a good time and playing some actual rugby. As well as playing friendlies, teams may also play in tournaments organised by touring companies.

School tour

Of a similar nature to club tours, depending on the funding available, schools may tour either domestically or abroad. Some schools in the UK organise international tours, visiting South Africa, Argentina, New Zealand or Australia and playing local schools, occasionally participating in tournaments.

Rugby tour companies

Here are some of the best companies to use for the perfect rugby tour.

Gullivers Sports Travel: *one of the very best when it comes to both supporter and playing tours, Gullivers have been in business since 1972 and have built an excellent reputation amongst both players and fans of the game (www.gulliverstravel.co.uk).*

Burleigh Travel: *based in Gloucestershire, Burleigh Travel operate a series of tours for all sports, for club, school and university teams, extending all over the world from Jersey to Fiji (www.burleightravel.co.uk).*

Tours 4 Sport: *with offices in Wales, Oxford and Manchester, Tours 4 Sport offer an extensive range of tours and tournaments for rugby teams (www.tours4sport.com).*

WHERE TO GO?

Picking a tour destination depends on the budget available and will essentially come down to domestic or overseas options:

Overseas tours

- **South Africa**: one of the greatest rugby nations in the world, South Africa has everything you need for the perfect rugby tour. An abundance of rugby teams spread across each of South Africa's provinces means that organising a tour abroad should not prove difficult, but traditionally tours normally take place around some of the country's biggest cities, such as Cape Town. There could also be the opportunity to see some of the world's most beautiful sights, including Table Mountain and Kruger National Park.

Essential stops: Cape Town, Port Elizabeth.

- **Argentina**: as love of the game grows in Latin America, Argentina is becoming one of the more popular destinations for rugby tours. Popular rugby bases are in Rosario and Buenos Aires, while sights to see include the Iguazu Falls and the Perito Moreno glacier in Patagonia.
  Essential stops: Buenos Aires, Rosario.

- **Barbados**: the rugby might not be of a similar standard, but Barbados offers one of the more aesthetically pleasing tours. With a series of activities ranging from surfing to water-skiing, or simply relaxing on the beach, a rugby tour of Barbados would be a truly unforgettable experience.
  Essential stop: Bridgetown.

Domestic tours

- **Ireland:** hopping over to the Emerald Isle keeps the budget low without taking away any of the intensity on the rugby field. Popular destinations include Dublin and Cork, while other rugby hotbeds include the region of Munster.
  Essential stop: Dublin.

- **Wales:** few countries are more passionate about their rugby than Wales, with hundreds of local clubs in the different regions. A tour of South Wales, for example, can be done easily at comparatively little cost, with an excellent post-match social agenda a necessity.
  Essential stop: Cardiff.

- **Scotland:** whether heading up to Melrose for its famous sevens tournament or to the capital, Edinburgh, Scotland makes a popular touring destination for many clubs.
  Essential stop: Edinburgh.

- **Cornwall:** in the far south-west of England, Cornwall has long been a hotbed of rugby and local pride in the game at county and club level runs high. As well as taking in some of England's best beaches and sights, touring teams will encounter home sides full of passionate support.

Essential stop: Penzance.

TOUR COURT

In a world without rules such as a rugby tour, order is established by a tour court, which seeks to try and punish any members of the touring party who commit a misdemeanour. Punishable offences on tour can range from turning up late for training to a poor vocal performance, or can even be based on reasons that lack any substance whatsoever.

SONG LIST

Before embarking on any rugby tour, players need to be familiar with the following rugby tour songs, as failure to do so could result in embarrassment as well as punishment.

- *The Wild Rover*: Irish by tradition, the song was penned in 1173 and has become popular in Irish pubs and rugby clubs around the world. A favourite on tour, slightly more crude variations of lyrics do exist, but have been deemed too offensive for print.

- *You've Lost That Lovin' Feeling*: a classic 60s smash hit from the Righteous Brothers, the *Top Gun* take on the song has become a social favourite during rugby evenings, with a passing female becoming the unsuspecting recipient of the serenade.

- *Jerusalem*: a William Blake poem converted into an English rugby anthem, Jerusalem is compulsory across the country, from Twickenham to your local clubhouse. A huge anthem to boost team spirit.

- *Wonderwall*: a tour classic, made essential by the victorious 1997 Lions Tour to South Africa, where it proved to be the soundtrack to their success. One for the masses and unifying a team on tour.

- *Yogi Bear:* one of the more crude songs sung on tour, based on the exploits of Yogi and his friends Suzy and Booboo.

Pocket fact H

As well as being a rugby legend, at the age of 12 Lawrence Dallaglio featured in his school choir that sang on the Tina Turner track We Don't Need Another Hero.

GEAR

Pranks and practical jokes are part of rugby tour life, so if you end up on the receiving end, acceptance is the easiest way to get through it. The following objects are more than likely to turn up on a rugby tour.

Duct tape

Not packed for its practical use, tape is taken along normally to leave a member of the touring party embarrassingly immobile in an unfortunate situation. A fine example is Ireland's touring bag man, Patrick 'Rala' O'Reilly, who, after a match against Wales, was taped to his duvet and left to go up and down in the hotel lift.

Clippers

Rather than being useful for fine-pruning or shaping acceptable haircuts, clippers are the cause of chaos on tour. Eyebrows, hair, legs and facial hair are all under threat from the mighty clippers.

Funnel

The standard drinking vessel of choice on a rugby tour, funnels are used for any form of drinking punishment. Made out of a typical kitchen funnel and long tube, the possibilities are endless.

Fancy dress

Whilst on tour, a minimum of at least two fancy dress nights are essential in order to scare off the locals and indicate to the wider world that you are indeed rugby tourists. There is no limit to the outrageousness of the attire, so be braced for the worst. The tour court must be responsible for overseeing that everyone obeys the fancy dress regulations, or punishment will result.

Humiliating costume

On every rugby tour there is an idiot of the week. The title might be awarded for messing up a potential scoring opportunity, losing a piece of essential kit, or waking up late for a flight and delaying the whole touring process. Inevitably, there is a special outfit for this esteemed position, and it could be anything from a penguin costume to a bin bag.

Tours are meant to be unforgettable as well as fun. Don't let yours be ruined by a night in the cells, in A&E, or in an airport because you have missed the flight home.

☺ RUGBY ON TV AND RADIO ☺

As the game's popularity has grown at both amateur and professional level, coverage has spread into the realms of books, film and television.

RADIO AND TV FIRSTS

- The first ever sports broadcast in the UK was a radio broadcast by the BBC, covering the rugby international match between England and Wales in 1927. The commentator for the match was Teddy Wakelam, a former captain of Harlequins. England won the game 11–9 at Twickenham.

Pocket fact H

Along with the broadcast by the BBC, the Radio Times *published a series of grids illustrating the pitch. The commentator would then refer to where the action was happening on the pitch, allowing readers to follow the flow of the game on their grid and visualise the match to greater effect.*

- The first ever televised rugby union match was in 1938, show-ing the Calcutta Cup match between England and Scotland at Twickenham, which England won by 21 points to 16 in front of a 70,000 crowd.

Pocket fact H

More than 15 million people in the UK watched Jonny Wilkinson win the World Cup for England in 2003 in the final against Australia.

GREATEST COMMENTATORS

Special moments in sport can be made by the perfect piece of commentary, with fans growing up with the familiar tones and catchphrases of legendary commentators. Here are some of the finest to have covered rugby.

Bill McLaren

Referred to as 'the voice of rugby', McLaren was the king of the rugby catchphrase. He played for Hawick RFC in Scotland but his playing career was ended after he contracted tuberculosis shortly before he would have won his first cap for Scotland.

His debut for BBC Radio came in 1953, covering an international match between Scotland and Wales. He would go on to commen-tate on rugby for the next 50 years, receiving a CBE for his servic-es to the game in 2003, as well as being inducted into the IRB's Hall of Fame in 2001. Fondly remembered and deeply missed, McLaren passed away in January 2010, but his love of the game and his contribution to it will not be forgotten.

Miles Harrison

Harrison has been the voice of Sky Sports rugby coverage since it began in 1994, and is instantly recognisable. He has covered four Lions tours, as well as multiple Heineken Cup finals, and com-mentated along with Sky partner Stuart Barnes for ITV during the 2007 Rugby World Cup.

Eddie Butler

A former Wales number 8 who won 16 caps for his country, six of them as captain, Butler began commentating with BBC Wales and now covers Six Nations matches for the BBC alongside Brian Moore. Popular for his Welsh tones, Butler also writes for the *Guardian* and *Observer* newspapers.

Grant Nisbett

Having commentated on rugby in New Zealand since 1984, 'Nisbo', as he is popularly known, has become a household name in the Land of the Long White Cloud. He has commentated on more than 200 Test matches and his experience is unrivalled. He often commentates alongside popular figures including Murray Mexted and Justin Marshall.

Hugh Bladen

South Africa's most famous rugby voice, Bladen has been a commentator for more than 35 years, firstly for SABC before moving to SuperSport in 1992. He has commentated on more than 150 Test matches.

☉ RUGBY WEBSITES ☉

With the growth of the internet over the last decade, rugby has embraced the surge in technology with many websites producing excellent, up-to-date content on a daily basis. Here are some of the best in the world.

THE RUGBY BLOG
www.therugbyblog.co.uk

Founded in 2007, The Rugby Blog is now one of the biggest of its kind, with a large, friendly community where there is always lots going on. From unique match previews and predictions to live updates, match reaction and feature articles, The Rugby Blog has it all – everyone has an opinion, and everyone is welcome to have their say.

RUGBYDUMP
www.rugbydump.com

Without doubt the best internet resource for the latest rugby video footage, rugbydump is based in South Africa and shows highlights from around the world. With an impressive following of more than 100,000 on Facebook, it continues to grow rapidly.

PLANET RUGBY
www.planetrugby.com

A must for breaking stories, Planet Rugby offers in-depth analysis of the latest matches along with a handy tipster column, for those looking to place a bet, and thorough match previews informing the reader of who to back.

GREEN & GOLD RUGBY
www.greenandgoldrugby.com

An Australian rugby-focused website first set up in 2007, Green & Gold is the leading Australian rugby blog and forum. It features an excellent podcast and expert views from former Australian World Cup-winning coach Bob Dwyer.

THE RUGBY FORUM
www.therugbyforum.com

A huge rugby community, the forum covers everything from international rugby to club rugby to rugby gaming.

ALTERNATIVE RUGBY COMMENTARY (ARC)
www.arcrugby.co.nz

Providing exactly what its name suggests, ARC is run by New Zealander Jed Thian, who has become famous for his humorous broadcasts from pubs around the world, from Chiswick to Auckland.

◉ RUGBY FILMS AND ◉ DOCUMENTARIES

Rugby's qualities of camaraderie, brotherhood and physical toil make the perfect recipe for a Hollywood blockbuster. Over the years there have been attempts to capture this essence and show-case it on the big screen. Meanwhile, certain matches have been preserved forever so that generations can relive these immortal moments.

FILMS

- *Alive* (1993): based on the true story of a plane that came down in the Andes when it was carrying a Uruguayan rugby team on tour, headed for Chile. The Stella Maris College's Old Christians rugby team crash in the mountains, and the leader-ship of captain Antonio Balbi comes to the fore as they seek a way out of their plight. The film is based on the book by Piers Paul Read and stars Ethan Hawke.

- *Murderball* (2005): a documentary film on the sport of wheelchair rugby, the film's gritty nature won over fans and critics alike with an insight into the intense rivalry between the Canadian and United States national Quad rugby teams. Using basic recording equipment and lighting, the film captures the sport as realistically as possible.

- *Forever Strong* (2008): with the tag line 'Life is a Contact Sport', *Forever Strong* is an all-American rugby movie based around the Highland rugby team in Utah. The film tells the story of a young rugby player who has gone off the rails and after serving a sentence in a juvenile detention centre, finds focus through playing for the Highland rugby team. The Maori heritage of the team is shown in the film through the use of the haka.

- *Invictus* (2009): another true story, *Invictus* captured the uni-fication of South Africa following the rugby team's success at the 1995 Rugby World Cup held in the country. Particularly focusing on the relationship between Nelson Mandela, played by Morgan Freeman, and Francois Pienaar, played by Matt Damon, the film was directed by Clint Eastwood and received many Oscar nominations, including nods for Freeman and Damon.

DOCUMENTARIES

- *Living With Lions* (1997): following the 1997 British & Irish Lions tour of South Africa, for the first time the public is invited into the world of a Lions tour, witnessing the whole spectrum of emotions, from the joy of winning to the despair of injuries. A humorous, unforgettable insight into rugby at the highest level.

- *Barbarians v All Blacks* (1973): billed as 'the greatest rugby match ever played', this DVD from the BBC recaptures the magic of the match played between the invitational Barbarians side against New Zealand, at Cardiff Arms Park on 27 January 1973.

- *Bill McLaren: Rugby at its best* (2002): released in 2002 with commentary from 'the voice of rugby', Bill McLaren looks back on some of rugby's finest players and moments, offering his views on the greatest players of all time.

◉ ESSENTIAL ANTHEMS ◉

When attending matches, certain songs have become integral to the occasion and the atmosphere. As well as knowing your anthems, take note and learn these other great rugby songs.

Swing Low, Sweet Chariot
Nearly always heard at Twickenham, *Swing Low, Sweet Chariot* has been sung at England games and at English rugby clubs for years. Originally composed by Wallis Willis, an African-American, in the mid-19th century, the gospel hymn has been linked to the England rugby teams since the late 1980s.

Pocket fact H

The song Swing Low, Sweet Chariot *was reputedly first sung at Twickenham by a group of students from the Douai School in Berkshire after debut winger Chris Oti scored a hat-trick against Ireland in 1988.*

Bread of Heaven or Cwm Rhondda
Often referred to as the Welsh rugby anthem, the popular hymn *Guide Me, O Thou Great Redeemer*, has become a staple of Wales international rugby matches both as a rousing anthem before kick-off and during the game. It was written by John Hughes and was first performed in 1907.

Flower of Scotland
This Scottish song written by Roy Williamson in 1967 has been used at Scotland's games as a rousing call. Sung with the accompaniment of a pipe band including bagpipes and drums it makes for an impressive performance.

Molly Malone
Adopted by the Irish national team, and Leinster, the traditional Irish folk song about a beautiful Irish girl from Dublin has become a favourite among rugby players.

Pocket fact H

A statue of Molly Malone can be found on the corner of Grafton Street and Suffolk Street in Dublin.

Hymns and Arias
Another Welsh favourite sung before kick-off and during matches in Cardiff, the song was originally written by Welsh singer and former coalminer Max Boyce in the 1970s. It was adapted by Welsh crowds to feature lyrics about travelling to Twickenham to see Wales play England.

The Fields of Athenry

Adopted by many Irish rugby teams, including the national team, Connacht, Munster and the London Irish rugby club in England, the Irish folk ballad recalls the Great Irish Famine but was written in the 1970s.

Delilah

Recorded and released by Welshman Tom Jones in 1968, the singer also performed this song before Wales defeated England at Wembley Stadium in 1999, and it has been adopted by Welsh rugby fans ever since. Easy to sing, even after a few pints.

Dirty Old Town

Another rousing Irish anthem which is a favourite in pubs around the world, the song was written by Ewen MacColl in 1949 and has become hugely popular. Sped up or performed at a slow tempo, versions have been sung by Rod Stewart, Paolo Nutini, U2 and The Pogues.

Pocket fact H

Hollywood movie star Javier Bardem played for the Spanish national team at youth level, first as a flanker and later as a prop.

GLOSSARY OF RUGBY TERMS

Rugby has a whole catalogue of terms that require an explanation, and some take a while to get to grips with. Here are some short explanations to help you get the hang of the lingo.

The 22
The area between the try line and the 22-metre line.

22 dropout
When play restarts with a drop kick from inside the defending team's 22.

All Blacks
The alternative name for the New Zealand national rugby team, which wears an entirely black kit.

Amateurism
A reference to rugby before 1995 in England, when professionalism was first introduced into the game. Amateurism means that players do not receive any form of payment for playing.

Backs
The group name for players wearing numbers 9 to 15, as well as 20, 21, 22 and occasionally 23. This group includes the scrum-half, fly-half, centres, wings and full-back.

Backfoot
Used for the offside rule, players can only enter rucks and mauls from the back foot of the player at the back, not from the side or in front of them.

Banana kick
A kick that curves in a banana shape. Used in open play or when taking penalty goals.

Biting
A serious offence where one player bites a part of another player's body. Standard punishment is a red card and extensive match ban.

Blood substitution
A replacement player is brought on when a team member is taken off temporarily in order to receive treatment for a cut or nose bleed before returning to the field. This is done to prevent the spread of infections like Aids and other diseases.

Boring in
An offence at the scrum, where props angle in when the scrums engage rather than pushing straight.

Cauliflower ears
A medical condition, this refers to the shape of the ears after the pressure on them from constant scrimmaging has caused blood clots, which make the ear shrivel and resemble a cauliflower.

Centre
The name of the two backs positioned between the fly-half and the wingers in the middle of the pitch. There are two types, inside centre, who wears the number 12 shirt, and outside centre, who wears the number 13.

Conversion
After a try is scored, teams may take a conversion when the team's kicker kicks the ball between the posts, for which two points are awarded.

Cross-field kick
A kick used in attack, when one player kicks the ball from one side of the pitch to the other, aiming either for open space or another player.

Dive pass
Normally performed under pressure by scrum-halves, who dive as they pass the ball, giving it added impetus.

Drop goal
Occurs when a player drop-kicks the ball through the posts, which can be done from anywhere on the field. Three points are awarded.

Drop kick
The kick by which drop goals are scored and the means of restarting the match from 22 dropouts and the half-way line at the start of each half or after someone has scored.

Dropping the bind
Players are not allowed to let go of their bind on the opposite man's shirt, otherwise the scrum will collapse.

Experimental Law Variations (ELVs)
Experimental Law Variations were introduced in 2009. Eight out of the 11 laws were added to the law book after the trial period.

Flanker
So called due to their positions on the flanks of the scrum. Renowned for their defence, flankers also lift and jump in the line-out. There are two types, the blindside flanker, positioned on the blind side of the scrum who wears number 6, and the openside flanker, who is on the open side of the scrum and wears number 7.

Fly-half
The key man on the field, a fly-half wears the number 10 shirt and is responsible in the main for passing and kicking. A fly-half tends to be the team's kicker, racking up the most points.

Forwards
The name for the group of players wearing numbers 1 to 8, as well as 16, 17, 18 and 19 and occasionally 20. The group includes the props, hooker, second rows, flankers and number 8.

Forward pass
A pass that goes forward as opposed to flat or backwards. The opposite team is awarded a scrum.

Fourth official
Positioned on the sidelines, the fourth official is in charge of substitutions.

Free kick
Awarded to teams for offences less severe than a penalty, teams can kick to touch (but do not retain possession), have a scrum, or tap the ball and run.

Front row
The row at the front of the scrum including the two props and the hooker.

Full-back
The last line of defence, full-backs are responsible for tackling and also catching high balls, as well as kicking the ball clear. They are commonly fast runners in attack, and occasionally also are the team's kicker. A full-back wears the number 15 shirt.

'Garryowen'
See 'up and under kick' below.

Gouging
A serious offence involving making contact with the eye which can blind or seriously injure. Results in a red card and a severe ban.

Grubber kick
An end-over-end kick, made by hitting the top of the ball with the toe of the boot.

High tackle
An illegal tackle around the neck or head. Players are penalised by the referee and can be issued with either a yellow or red card, depending on the severity of the tackle.

Hooker
Positioned in between the two props, it is the hooker's job to hook the ball backwards in the scrum towards his team. They are also responsible for throwing the ball into the lineout. Hookers wear the number 2 shirt.

International Rugby Board (IRB)
The IRB is the game's governing body in charge of regulating laws from discipline to organising tournaments, including the World Cup.

In-goal area
The area behind the posts between the try line and the dead-ball line.

Irish Rugby Football Union (IRFU)
The governing body of the game in Ireland.

Knock-on
When the ball goes forward off a player's hand or arm. A scrum is awarded to the opposing team.

Lineout
When the ball goes out of play into touch, a team takes a lineout, using up to three jumpers, at the front, middle and back of the lineout, working in pods of two lifters and one jumper. The ball is thrown in from the side and the lifters will lift the designated jumper who will attempt to take the ball cleanly. In order to confuse the opposition so that they cannot compete for the ball, jumpers and lifters may move up and down the line before the ball is thrown in.

Lions
The shortened name for the British & Irish Lions, an invitational side who tour Australia, South Africa and New Zealand every four years.

Mark
Players can call a mark when catching the ball from a kick in their 22. Calling the mark prevents the opposition from tackling the man.

Maul
Formed either from a lineout or in open play, mauls happen when a group of attacking players bind together and drive forward, with the ball positioned with the man at the back of the maul. Players can only join from the back of the maul on both sides, and it is illegal to pull the maul down while it is moving.

Mouthguard
A piece of ethylene-vinyl acetate moulded to the shape of a player's teeth to protect the teeth and jaw.

National Provincial Championship (NPC)
The domestic league tournament held in New Zealand, now replaced by the ITM Cup.

Number 8
Positioned at the back of the scrum, the number 8 also either lifts or jumps in the lineout. Number 8s wear the shirt that their name suggests.

Pass
Players make many types of passes: see dive pass, pop pass, and spin pass.

Penalty
Awarded after one team commits an offence. The opposition has four options from a penalty: kicking for the posts (if within the kicker's range), a scrum, a kick to touch, or running the ball (by tapping the ball with the foot).

Penalty try
Awarded to a team when a certain or likely try is prevented from being scored due to an offence. The conversion is taken from in front of the posts.

Pods
Used in lineouts, featuring two lifters and one jumper.

Pop pass
Carried out by flicking the ball into the air with the fingers.

Professionalism
When players are paid in exchange for playing and signing contracts. Globally introduced in 1995 after the Rugby World Cup.

Prop
Used primarily in the scrum and lineout. The loosehead prop, who wears the number 1 shirt, is positioned on the left side of the scrum, while the tighthead prop (wearing number 3) goes in the space between the opposition's hooker and loosehead prop. Props are also used in the lineout to lift jumpers, given their considerable strength.

Quick throw-in
The term used for a quick lineout, where if the ball has gone out and a player gets to it before the lineout forms. The ball is then thrown in five metres and play continues.

Red card
Issued for a serious offence. If a red card is shown to a player then they must leave the field immediately. A player can also be awarded a red card if he receives two yellow cards in the match.

Ruck
A ruck is formed when a tackled player is on the ground and players from both sides bind, standing over him in order to force the opposition off and secure the ball. Players must enter from the backfoot, and cannot enter from the side. Once the ruck is formed, players must not use their hands to retrieve the ball.

Rugby Football Union (RFU)
The governing body for rugby in England and the first of its kind in the world, formed in 1871.

Rugby league
The name of the game formed by the Northern Rugby Union following the split from the RFU, it is played predominantly in the north of England, as well as in New Zealand, Australia, France and Wales. It is played with 13 men instead of rugby union's 15.

Rugby School
The school in Rugby, Warwickshire, from which the sport takes its name. According to legend it was here where schoolboy William Webb Ellis, playing football, first picked up the ball and ran with it, creating the game of rugby.

Rugby sevens
A shortened version of the 15-man game, rugby sevens features seven players playing on the same-sized pitch for halves lasting either seven or 10 minutes.

Rugby union
Created in the 19th century, rugby union is now played in 108 countries around the world. Teams are made up of 15 players,

with the team that scores the most points from tries, penalties, conversions and drop goals winning the match.

Rugby World Cup
The global tournament held every four years featuring 20 teams competing to become world champions.

SANZAR
The abbreviation for the southern hemisphere governing body, with representation from South Africa (SA), New Zealand (NZ) and Australia (AR). They are in charge of organising the Four Nations and Super Rugby tournaments.

Scottish Rugby Union (SRU)
The governing body for rugby in Scotland.

Scrum
Used to restart the game after a knock-on, forward pass or from penalties and free kicks, scrums see the two sets of forwards linking with each other and driving over the ball to decide possession.

Scrum-half
Wearing the number 9 shirt, scrum-halves are often the shortest but also among the quickest players on the field. They are responsible for communicating between the forwards and the backs, as well as distribution from rucks, mauls, scrums and lineouts.

Second row
Often the tallest players on the pitch, the second rows take their name from being in the second row of the scrum. They are also commonly the main jumpers and organisers in the lineout.

Shoulder charge
An illegal tackle where the player takes down his opponent without wrapping his arms around the man.

Sidestep
Where a player motions one way before jinking in the other direction, confusing his opponent.

Sin-bin
A term referring to when a player has to sit on the sidelines for 10 minutes following a yellow card – 'being sent to the sin-bin'.

Spear tackle
When a player following contact drops the tackled player to the ground on either their neck or head. Incredibly dangerous, it can result in serious injury for the tackled player. The perpetrator is usually sent off and banned.

Spin pass
The most common pass in the game, a spin pass makes the flight of the ball cleaner and easier for the recipient to catch.

Springboks
The alternative name for the South African national rugby team, referring to the springbok, an antelope indigenous to the country.

Stamping
Where a player on the ground is struck repeatedly by the studs from a player's boot, in order to either clear from the ruck or seriously injure. It is a foul that can result in severe punishment from the referee.

Substitution
Either put into effect as a result of an injury or tactically, substitutions see the swapping of one player on the field for a replacement. Players can be brought back on, especially in the front rows. See also 'blood substitution'.

Tackle
A tackle happens when a defender wraps their arms around the attacker, from the chest down to the ankles, and drives him to the ground using the shoulder. See also 'high tackle' and 'spear tackle'.

Television Match Official (TMO)
A TMO can ascertain whether a try has been scored or not with the use of slow-motion replays.

Test match
Another name for an international match between two sides played outside of a tournament.

Touchline
The line on the sides of the field. When the balls passes these lines, it is in touch, and a lineout or restart is taken depending where on the pitch the ball has gone out of play.

Touch judge
Also known as a linesman, touch judges mark where the ball has gone out of play, as well assisting the referee in identifying offences committed by either team.

Touch rugby
A form of the game where tackling and kicking are not allowed. Players must pass the ball when they are touched.

Truck-and-trailer
A technical term to describe when a maul has become fractured, when the player with the ball is not connected to the rest of the forwards driving in front of him. It results in a penalty to the opposition.

Try
The means by which the most points can be scored. Tries are scored when the ball is placed or touched down over the opposition's try line by the attacking team. A try is worth five points and is followed immediately by a conversion attempt.

Up and under kick
A high kick hoisted up by the fly-half, otherwise known as a 'Garryowen'.

Wallabies
The alternative name for the Australia national team, referring to the native animal.

Welsh Rugby Union (WRU)
The governing body of the game in Wales.

Wingers
Positioned on the far sides of the field, wingers are normally the quickest players and score more tries than any other position. They wear shirt numbers 11 and 14.